easy smoothies
& juices

easy smoothies & juices

simply delicious recipes for goodness in a glass

RYLAND
PETERS
& SMALL
LONDON NEW YORK

Senior Designer Iona Hoyle
Editor Rebecca Woods
Picture Research Emily Westlake
Production Maria Petalidou
Art Director Leslie Harrington
Publishing Director Alison Starling
Indexer Hilary Bird

First published in 2011
by Ryland Peters & Small
20–21 Jockey's Fields
London WC1R 4BW
and
Ryland Peters & Small, Inc.
519 Broadway, 5th Floor
New York NY10012

www.rylandpeters.com

10 9 8 7 6 5 4 3 2 1

UK ISBN 978 1 84975 108 7
US ISBN 978 1 84975 109 4

A CIP record for this book is available
from the British Library.

US CIP data has been applied for

Printed in China

Notes

• All spoon measurements are level
unless otherwise specified.

• Weights and measurements have
been rounded up or down slightly to
make measuring easier.

• All yoghurt is plain unless otherwise
specified.

• When using slices of citrus fruit in a
drink, try to find organic or unwaxed
fruits and wash well before using. If you
can only find treated fruits, scrub well
in warm water and rinse before using.

• To sterilize cordial bottles, wash them
in hot, soapy water and rinse in boiling
water. Place in a large saucepan and
cover with hot water. With the saucepan
lid on, bring the water to a boil and
continue boiling for 15 minutes. Turn
off the heat and leave the bottles in the
hot water until just before they are to
be filled. Invert the bottles onto a clean
dish towel to dry. Sterilize the lids for
5 minutes, by boiling or according to
the manufacturer's instructions. Bottles
should be filled and sealed while they
are still hot.

For digital editions visit
www.rylandpeters.com/apps.php

contents

introduction

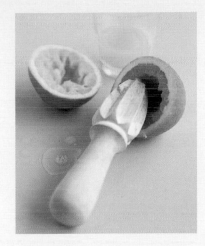

Whether it's a quick breakfast on the go, a refreshing thirst quencher on a hot day, a vitamin boost when you are feeling run down or a party tipple, there is sure to be a smoothie or juice that's perfect for the occasion.

Smoothies and juices are one of the most wonderful, tasty ways to boost your intake of vitamins and fibre. Therefore, many of the recipe introductions in this book will give you a quick summary of the health benefits of each drink. Fruit Smoothies and Vegetable Juices are blended with the whole fruit or vegetable and are packed with fibre, or for a lighter drink, try one of the Fruit Juices & Coolers. But not all these drinks are designed with health in mind. For a little decadence, turn straight to Dairy Smoothies to find some less angelic alternatives, or to Fruit with a Kick for some very adult variations.

If you grow your own fruit and vegetables, or simply like to hunt out bargains at local markets, smoothies and juices are also the perfect way to use up a glut of any produce you may have. And, although there is sure to be something for everyone within this bountiful collection, smoothies are so easily adaptable that you can customise any of the recipes to your own taste, or to what is available seasonally.

From traditional recipes, such as Banana & Strawberry Smoothie, to more original inclusions, such as Avocado, Pear & Mint Cooler or Chai Vanilla Milkshake, *Easy Smoothies & Juices* includes 150 recipes for delicious treats to drink. Smoothies and juices couldn't be easier or quicker to make, or more enjoyable to consume!

fruit smoothies

Bananas and papayas don't juice effectively – their pulp is too dense – but they are definitely candidates for the blender treatment. If your blender doesn't crush ice, add it at the end, but to help the machine run, you may need to add a little yoghurt or water.

banana & papaya smoothie

1 small papaya, peeled, deseeded and cut into chunks
1 banana, peeled and cut into chunks
about 6 ice cubes
125 ml/½ cup yoghurt or water, plus extra if needed
1 tablespoon wheatgerm (optional)

serves 2–4

Put the papaya and banana in a blender with the ice and water or yoghurt, if using. Blend until smooth, then add the wheatgerm, if using, and extra yoghurt or water to form a pourable consistency. Serve immediately.

variation
Blueberries and banana make a famous combination. Blend them with ice, yoghurt and a dash of honey.

This is a lovely healthy drink to start your day – freshly ground linseed is great for the skin and is also rich in fibre. Tahini is a rich source of calcium, important for healthy teeth, bones and hair, and contains good fats, which also help nourish the skin. Oat bran should be avoided by those with gluten sensitivities, but can be replaced with a tablespoon of sunflower seeds.

kick-start your day

1 tablespoon linseed/flaxseed
1 small mango, about 400 g/14 oz.
1 banana
2 tablespoons oat bran
1 tablespoon tahini
250 ml/1 cup sheep's milk yoghurt
250 ml/1 cup sheep's milk

serves 2

Crush the linseed/flaxseed using a pestle and mortar or spice grinder. To prepare the mango, slice down each side of the stone and cut away the flesh from the skin. Peel and slice the banana. Put the fruit in a blender with the ground linseed/flaxseed, oat bran and tahini and blend for 30 seconds. Add the yoghurt and milk and blend until smooth.

Unlike most fruit, avocado has a high fat content, but it is monounsaturated fat, so will not raise cholesterol levels. Avocados are also rich in lecithin and minerals, making them great brain food. The addition of mint adds a refreshing quality to the drink, and this aromatic herb also calms the digestive tract and helps quell nausea.

avocado, pear & mint cooler

1 avocado
500 ml/2 cups pear juice
leaves from 4 sprigs of mint
freshly squeezed juice of 1 lime

serves 2–3

Cut the avocado in half and remove the stone. Scoop out the flesh, put in a blender with the pear juice, mint and lime juice and blend until smooth.

LEFT *kick-start your day*
RIGHT *avocado, pear & mint cooler*

dried pear & mint froth

This marvellous cooler with sweet pears and refreshing mint is perfect for a sunny summer morning. It is best served ice cold.

Dried fruit smoothies make life easy when there isn't a single piece of fresh fruit left in the bowl. Just pop the dried fruit in a glass, cover with water and leave in the refrigerator overnight. Next morning you have your delicious high-fibre fruit hit all ready for the blender.

dried pear & mint froth

6 dried pears
leaves from 6 sprigs of mint
6 ice cubes (optional)

serves 1

Put the pears in a glass, cover with water and chill for 4 hours or overnight. When ready to serve, put in a blender with the mint. Add the soaking water and blend to a froth. If preferred, blend ice cubes with the other ingredients to make an icy froth, adding extra water if too thick.

breakfast shake with dried apricots

6–8 dried apricots
6 ice cubes
honey, to taste (optional)

serves 1

Put the apricots in a glass and cover with cold water. Chill for about 4 hours or overnight. When ready to use, discard the stones if any, then transfer the apricots and soaking water to a blender. Add the ice cubes and blend to a thick shake. Taste and add a little honey if preferred.

This naturally sweet blend of fruits makes a delicious smoothie combination that is rich in vitamin C – it will bring a smile to your face and balance to both your immune system and your bowels!

frozen berry & banana blend

1 banana
200 g/1⅔ cups frozen mixed berries
250 ml/1 cup apple juice
2 scoops berry sorbet

serves 2

Peel and chop the banana. Put in a blender with all the other ingredients and blend until smooth.

A lovely balance of vitamin C-rich flavours. Include some of the white orange pith as it contains not only fibre but bioflavonoids, which enhance the absorption of vitamin C found in the juice. If you don't have a juicer, use 100 ml/scant ½ cup each of organic apple and orange juice instead of the whole fruits.

fruit bowl frappé

2 apples
2 oranges
1 banana
250 g/2 cups frozen strawberries
8 ice cubes

serves 2

Quarter the apples and cut in half again if large. Peel the oranges, leaving some of the pith intact, and cut the flesh into chunks. Press the apples and oranges through a juicer into a jug/pitcher.

Peel and chop the banana. Put in a blender with the apple and orange juice, strawberries and ice cubes and blend until smooth.

LEFT TO RIGHT

frozen berry & banana blend

fruit bowl frappé

blueberry buzz (recipe on page 19)

berry boost

This colourful thick juice is a boost indeed, packed full of vitamin C, antioxidants and bioflavonoids. Cranberry juice is great for urinary-tract infections such as cystitis, but beware of added sugars. If you can find fresh cranberries, add a handful to the blender and complete the recipe with 250 ml/1 cup apple juice instead of the cranberry juice.

berry boost

125 g/1 cup frozen blueberries

125 g/1 cup frozen raspberries

125 g/1 cup frozen strawberries

250 ml/1 cup cranberry juice

serves 2–3

Put all the ingredients in a blender and blend until smooth.

The blueberries and cranberry juice combine to great effect in this refreshing drink. It is simple but delicious and nutritious, especially if you use organic, sugar-free cranberry juice, available from good health-food stores.

blueberry buzz

250 g/2 cups frozen blueberries

250 ml/1 cup cranberry juice

serves 2

Put the blueberries and cranberry juice in a blender and blend until smooth.

pictured on page 17

Not only a delicious and nutritious ingredient alone, oranges will also help to extend more expensive fruits, such as blueberries, and their gentle acidity develops the flavour.

blueberry & orange smoothie

freshly squeezed juice of 4 oranges
1 punnet/basket blueberries, about 250 g/2 cups
sugar, to taste (optional)

serves 1–2

Put the orange juice in a blender, add the blueberries and blend until smooth. Add sugar to taste, if preferred.

Alternatively, peel the oranges, then feed half of them through a juicer, followed by the blueberries, then the remaining oranges.

Apricots are very dense, so you may like to pulp them in the blender rather than putting them through the juicer. If you do decide to juice, remove the skins first, and juice them alternately with pieces of apple.

berry, apricot & orange slush

8 ripe apricots, halved and stoned, then coarsely chopped
8 strawberries, hulled and halved
freshly squeezed juice of 2 oranges

serves 1

Put the apricots, strawberries and orange juice in a blender and purée until smooth, adding water if needed. (If the mixture is too thick, add a few ice cubes and blend again.)

note
To remove the apricot skins, bring a saucepan of water to the boil, then blanch the apricots for about 1 minute. When cool enough to handle, remove the skin with the back of a knife.

LEFT *blueberry & orange smoothie*
RIGHT *berry, apricot & orange slush*

In summer, when fruit is good quality, plentiful and relatively inexpensive, make this fruity mixture in bigger quantities for a party. Take care with your choice of fruit though – keep it red, orange and yellow as if you add green fruits you'll spoil the colour. It's delicious made with mineral water, but you could use cherryade for a children's party. If the fruit is sweet and ripe, you may not need any sugar or honey.

summer fruit crush
with peach, nectarine, apricots & raspberries

1 ripe peach, peeled and halved

1 ripe nectarine, halved

2 ripe apricots, halved

a handful of raspberries

6 ice cubes

sparkling mineral water, to taste

honey or sugar (optional)

serves 2

Discard the stones from the fruit. Put all the fruit in a blender, add the ice and enough mineral water to make the blades run. Blend to a purée. Add honey or sugar to taste, then enough extra water to produce the consistency you like. Pour into glasses and serve.

This adaptable drink is delicious served cooled with ice or as a virgin mulled wine – warm it over a low heat (without the ice cubes) for a nourishing and sustaining drink, especially if the autumn nights are starting to feel chilly.

autumn classic

4 apples
300 g/2¼ cups frozen blackberries
1 tablespoon maple syrup
or soft brown sugar
a pinch of ground cinnamon
6 ice cubes

serves 2–3

Cut the apples into pieces and press through a juicer into a jug/pitcher. Pour the juice into a blender and add the remaining ingredients. Blend until smooth.

Super-rich in vitamin C, this is a great iron tonic. Cherries are much higher in vitamin C than citrus fruits and other berries, so this drink is also an excellent cold cure. If you can't find frozen cherries, use bottled cherries in natural syrup.

cherry berry crush

300 g/2¼ cups frozen stoned cherries
125 g/1 cup frozen raspberries
1 tablespoon soft brown sugar

serves 2

Put all the ingredients in a blender and blend until really smooth.

cherry berry crush

Peaches aren't tropical fruits, but they go very well with coconut milk in this rich, decadent-tasting smoothie. Other fruit such as apricots, mangoes, bananas or papaya may be used instead of the peaches.

coconut milk smoothie
with vanilla, peaches & lime

4 large, ripe peaches, peeled, halved, stoned and cut into wedges

250 ml/1 cup canned coconut milk

a few drops of vanilla extract

2 tablespoons sugar, or to taste

6 ice cubes

freshly squeezed juice and zest of 1 lime, cut into long shreds

serves 2

Put the peaches in a blender, add the coconut milk, vanilla, sugar, lime juice and ice cubes and blend until smooth. Taste and add extra sugar if necessary.

Serve in chilled glasses, topped with the shreds of lime zest.

The name of this drink references Australia's most famous beach. After all, there are few better ways of watching the world go by than sipping fruit shakes as the heat of the day fades and the sun worshippers head home for the night.

bondi rip

1 large mango, peeled, stoned and diced
1 banana, peeled and sliced
250 ml/1 cup pineapple juice
50 ml/¼ cup raspberry syrup
6 ice cubes

serves 2

Put the mango, banana and pineapple juice in a blender. Add the ice cubes and whizz until smooth.

To serve, drizzle a little raspberry syrup down the sides of 2 tall glasses, pour in the blended fruit and ice mixture and stir well. Serve immediately.

A delicious blend of flavours, and a nutritious and tasty drink is a prescription in a glass! Much is written about coconut milk being bad for you due to its high fat content, but in fact its high levels of lauric acid will help you lose or maintain weight, reduce the risk of heart disease, lower your cholesterol and rejuvenate your skin to help keep you looking younger.

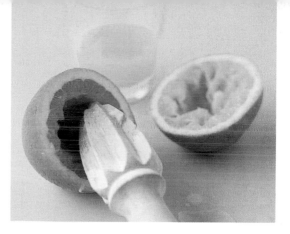

spiced mango, coconut & lime smoothie

1 large mango, about 550 g/1 lb. 4 oz.
400 ml/1¾ cups canned coconut milk
freshly squeezed juice of 1 lime
250 ml/1 cup freshly squeezed
orange juice
½ teaspoon ground allspice

serves 4

To prepare the mango, slice down each side of the stone and cut away the flesh from the skin. Put the flesh in a blender with the coconut milk, lime juice, orange juice and allspice and blend until smooth.

Strawberries and mango are a lovely combination: the scent of the strawberries lifts the flavour of the mango in a delicious fashion. Soy milk adds a sweet creaminess to this smoothie and makes it a great vegan option, although it is sure to be enjoyed by all.

mango smoothie
with strawberries & soy milk

6 ice cubes
500 g/1 lb 2 oz. fresh or canned mango pieces
12 large strawberries, hulled and halved
freshly squeezed juice of 1 lemon
250 ml/1 cup soy milk, or to taste

serves 4

Put the ice cubes in a blender and blend to a snow. Add the mango pieces, strawberries and lemon juice, and then pour in the soy milk with the machine running.

Add extra soy milk or water until the mixture is the thickness of single/light cream. Transfer to a chilled jug/pitcher and serve in tall glasses.

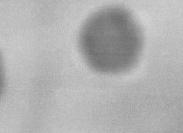

This pretty, vibrantly coloured drink is perfect for a pre-dinner drink on a balmy summer evening, with the hint of passion fruit adding a wonderfully exotic feel.

mango & berry pash

100 g/scant 1 cup frozen mixed berries, thawed
1 tablespoon icing/confectioners' sugar
1 large mango, peeled and stoned
(about 250 g/9 oz. flesh)
1 passion fruit, halved
sparkling mineral water, to top up
ice cubes, to serve

serves 2

Put the berries in a bowl and stir in the icing/confectioners' sugar, mashing well with a fork. Set aside for 15 minutes, then pass through a fine sieve/strainer. Purée the mango flesh in a blender or liquidizer until smooth. Scoop out the passion fruit pulp and stir into the mango purée.

Put a few ice cubes into 2 tall glasses, add the berry mixture and mango and passion fruit purée and top up with sparkling mineral water to serve.

A native of Asia, ginger has both culinary and medicinal values – its distinctive tang adds a wonderful flavour and 'kick' to foods, while its healing properties include aiding digestion and even reducing cholesterol levels. Papaya also helps digestion, and the melon is both cooling and hydrating. Take this drink without food, as melon tends to ferment some foods in the stomach, causing bloating.

papaya, melon & pear digestive

1 small papaya, about 350 g/12 oz.

400 g/14 oz. cantaloupe melon

250 ml/1 cup pear juice

freshly squeezed juice of 1 large lime

1 teaspoon grated fresh ginger

serves 2

Peel the papaya and cut it in half, scoop out and discard the seeds and then chop the flesh. Chop the melon. Put the papaya and melon in a blender and add the remaining ingredients. Blend until smooth.

LEFT to RIGHT *watermelon & raspberry surprise,
morning cleanser, bananarama (recipe on page 133)*

The surprise here is the curious yet exotic flavour of rosewater – it's quite intriguing. This is a particularly refreshing morning drink that satisfies the senses as well as the stomach. Watermelon is both cooling and hydrating, while rosewater is uplifting, a stress reliever and soothes the nerves.

watermelon & raspberry surprise

large wedge watermelon, about
1 kg/2 lb. 4 oz.
150 g/1¼ cups fresh or frozen
raspberries
1 tablespoon rosewater

serves 3

Deseed the watermelon, then cut the flesh into chunks. Put in a blender with the raspberries and rosewater and blend until smooth.

Mornings are not always about get-up-and-go and we often feel the need to detox, especially after a late night of over-indulgence! Pears are very cleansing and cucumber is about the best diuretic around – this combination is perfect for cleaning the system. With the addition of grapefruit, which aids the body in overcoming alcohol intoxication, you can say goodbye to your hangover.

morning cleanser

4 firm ripe pears, about 650 g/1 lb. 7 oz.
½ cucumber
1 small grapefruit
5 cm/2 inch piece fresh ginger

serves 2

Cut the pears and cucumber into chunks. Peel the grapefruit and cut into wedges. Press everything through a juicer into a jug/pitcher.

There's plenty of fibre, vitamin C and energy in this lovely drink. If you're in a hurry, substitute 250 ml/1 cup each of pear and orange juice for the whole fruits and make this drink using just a blender.

orange, pear & banana breeze

2 pears

2 oranges

1 banana

8 ice cubes

serves 2

Cut the pears into chunks. Peel the oranges and cut the flesh into pieces. Press the pear and orange pieces through a juicer into a jug/pitcher and then pour the juice into a blender. Peel and chop the banana and add it to the blender with the ice cubes. Blend until smooth.

The melon, cucumber and lime make this a hydrating and detoxifying drink. It has an added kick of spicy ginger to increase circulation. Ginger in any form is a great remedy for nausea.

melon, cucumber & sweet ginger frappé

½ galia melon, about 1 kg/2 lb. 4 oz.

½ cucumber

freshly squeezed juice of ½ lime

1 tablespoon chopped stem ginger

1 tablespoon ginger syrup from the jar

6 ice cubes

serves 2

Deseed the melon, scoop the flesh from the skin and put in a blender. Peel and chop the cucumber and add to the blender with the remaining ingredients. Blend until smooth.

melon, cucumber & sweet ginger frappé

Like all berries, raspberries are a valuable source of antioxidants. Frozen raspberries are useful for juices, because if a raspberry is at its peak, you really just want to pop it into your mouth and enjoy it neat! Frozen raspberries are often far cheaper too. Lychee juice is traditionally used to alleviate a cough and ulcers in the stomach. Use lychees in natural juice if you can find them.

raspberry, apple & lychee smoothie

200 g/1⅓ cups frozen raspberries
565 g/1 lb. 5 oz. canned lychees, drained and deseeded
250 ml/1 cup apple juice

serves 2

Put all the ingredients in a blender and then blend until smooth.

This fruit concoction is an excellent digestive aid best drunk half an hour before you eat or as a refreshing, cooling drink on a hot summer's day. It is excellent for morning sickness in pregnancy or any time when feeling nauseous as ginger helps break down undigested food and quell nausea.

These delicious stone fruits are at their best when bought in season for their aromatic and nutritional qualities. They are rich in antioxidants and vitamin C, especially when combined with orange juice. A great drink to aid against anaemia and ward off colds and flu.

pineapple, ginger & mint slushie

½ small pineapple, about 850 g/1 lb. 14 oz.
1 teaspoon peeled and grated fresh ginger
leaves from 2 sprigs of fresh mint
8 ice cubes

serves 2

Peel the pineapple and remove the tough central core. Roughly chop the flesh and put in a blender with the ginger, mint and ice. Blend until smooth.

peach, apricot & plum fizz

1 peach
1 plum
2 apricots
125 ml/½ cup freshly squeezed orange juice
8 ice cubes

serves 2

Halve the peach, plum and apricots and discard the stones. Roughly chop the flesh, put in a blender with the orange juice and ice and blend until smooth.

LEFT *pineapple, ginger & mint slushie*
RIGHT *peach, apricot & plum fizz*

A delicious fruit smoothie based on the sharbat – the beautiful sweetened fruit drink created for the imperial courts of Muslim rulers from Persia to Moorish Spain, from the Holy Land to Moghul India. Because Muslims don't drink alcohol and many of their lands are deserts, they have created an amazing array of non-alcoholic thirst-quenching drinks. This is, of course, the origin of our word 'sherbet'.

pineapple ginger smoothie

2.5 cm/1 inch piece fresh ginger, peeled and grated
1 pineapple, peeled, cored and chopped
sugar or sugar syrup, to taste
ice cubes, to taste

serves 4

Working in batches if necessary, put the ginger in a blender, add the pineapple and blend to a smooth purée, adding enough cold water to make the blades run. Taste and add sugar or sugar syrup to taste. Half-fill a jug/pitcher with ice cubes, pour over the pineapple mixture, stir and serve.

Alternatively, add about 10 ice cubes when blending the ginger and pineapple.

A delicious combination of tropical fruit flavours. When choosing a pineapple, pull one of the outside leaves; if ripe, it will pull away easily. The more wrinkled a passion fruit, the riper its flesh. About 8 large passion fruit will yield 250 ml/1 cup of pulp. Passion fruit pulp is also available in cans from large supermarkets.

pineapple & passion fruit soy shake

½ pineapple
250 ml/1 cup passion fruit pulp
250 ml/1 cup soy milk
4 scoops vanilla soy ice cream

serves 3

Peel the pineapple, discard the tough central core and chop the flesh. Put it in a blender with the passion fruit pulp, soy milk and ice cream. Blend until smooth.

You may find the inclusion of a savoury ingredient such as tahini (sesame seed paste) strange in a smoothie, but it makes a delicious drink. Tahini helps boost calcium levels.

banana, sesame & maple soy smoothie

1 banana
2 tablespoons tahini
2 tablespoons maple syrup
300 ml/1¼ cups soy milk
250 ml/1 cup soy yoghurt

serves 2

Peel the banana, chop the flesh and put in a blender with the remaining ingredients. Blend until smooth.

LEFT *pineapple & passion fruit soy shake*
RIGHT *banana, sesame & maple soy smoothie*

When you buy soy milk, always read the label. Many of the nutrients in soy are destroyed during processing into milk, so most manufacturers fortify their products with additional vitamins such as B$_{12}$ as well as calcium. Buy genetically modified organism-free, organic soy milk with no added sugar, sweeteners or vegetable oils.

raspberry smoothie with soy milk

150 g/1¼ cups raspberries
about 500 ml/2 cups soy milk
12 ice cubes
honey, to taste

serves 4

Put the raspberries*, soy milk and ice cubes in a blender and purée to a froth. Serve the honey separately so people can sweeten to taste.

*note**
If you love raspberries, you can reserve a few and sprinkle on top of each glass before serving.

This is a very good way of making one mango go just a little further. You can also freeze the mixture into gorgeous frozen lollipops to have later in the day.

strawberry slush
with mango & lime

1 ripe mango, peeled, stoned and chopped, or 1 small can unsweetened mango pieces

grated zest and freshly squeezed juice of 1 lime

6 large strawberries, hulled and halved

6 ice cubes

sparkling mineral water

honey or sugar, to taste (optional)

serves 1–2

Put the mango in a blender. Add the grated lime zest and juice, strawberries and ice cubes and blend to a froth. Add enough mineral water to make the blades run and to make the mixture the consistency you prefer. Add honey or sugar, if using, then serve.

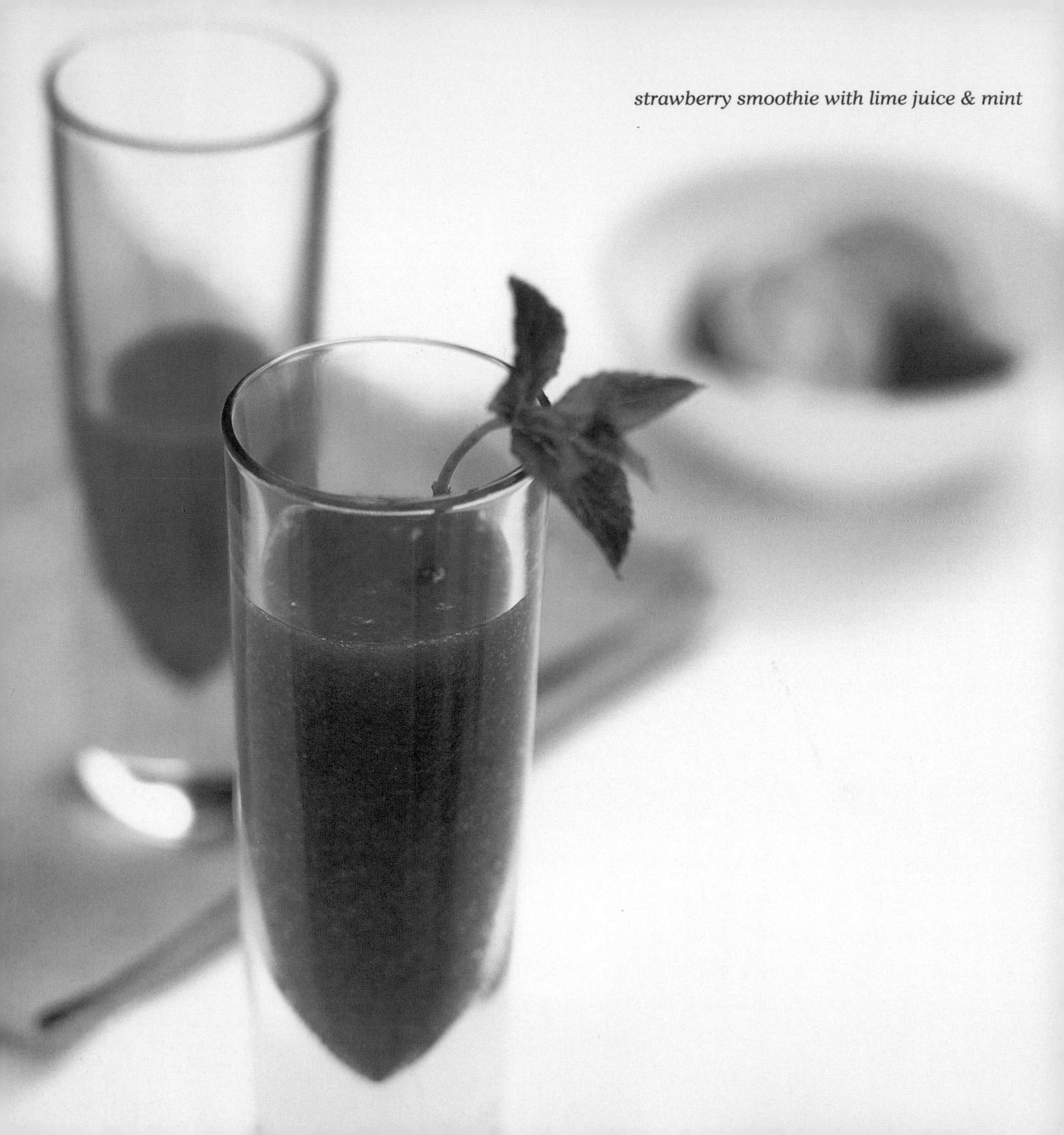

strawberry smoothie with lime juice & mint

A marvellous way to be absolutely self-indulgent. One punnet of strawberries should last you two days – or one day if you're being generous and making a smoothie for someone else. The rule with strawberries is to wash them before hulling (removing the green frill and stalk) – otherwise they fill with water and you get a more watery strawberry.

When choosing mangoes, squeeze them lightly; they should yield a little without feeling squishy and have a fragrant, even heady aroma. If you can find them, buy the Alphonso mango (from India): it is magnificent. This drink calls for fresh rather than frozen strawberries to complement the wonderfully sweet flavour of the mango.

strawberry smoothie with lime juice & mint

about 6 large ripe strawberries
(about ½ punnet/basket), hulled

4–6 ice cubes

freshly squeezed juice of 1 lime

6 fresh mint leaves, plus 1 sprig to serve

honey or sugar, to taste (optional)

serves 1

Put the ice cubes in a blender and work to a snow. Add the strawberries and blend until smooth.

Add the lime juice, mint and sugar or honey, if preferred. Blend again and serve, topped with a sprig of mint.

mango & strawberry delight

2 mangoes

250 g/2 cups strawberries

ice cubes, to serve

serves 2

Cut down each side of the mango stone and scoop the flesh from the skin and put in a blender. Hull the strawberries, add to the mango and blend until smooth. Serve over ice.

pictured on page 57

Guava is richer in vitamin C than most citrus fruits and is also packed with vitamins A and B. If you like you can make this drink without using a blender, by crushing the ice cubes by hand with an ice crusher, or putting them in a plastic bag and bashing them with a rolling pin. Then mix the juices with the crushed ice.

guava, strawberry & apple refresher

4 apples
250 g/2 cups strawberries
200 ml/¾ cup guava nectar
12 ice cubes

serves 2–3

Cut the apples into chunks and hull the strawberries. Press the apple pieces and strawberries through a juicer into a jug/pitcher. Pour the juice into a blender and add the guava nectar and ice. Blend until smooth.

This is a detox tonic, as grapefruit juice significantly increases the production and activity of liver detoxification enzymes. For extra bioflavonoid activity, keep the pith on the grapefruit to aid vitamin C absorption. If you don't have a juicer, substitute 300 ml/1¼ cups freshly squeezed grapefruit juice for the whole grapefruit.

frozen cranberry, raspberry & grapefruit slushie

3 ruby grapefruit
300 ml/1¼ cups cranberry juice
4 scoops raspberry sorbet

serves 2

Peel the grapefruit, retaining some of the pith, cut the flesh into chunks and press through a juicer. Pour into a blender, add the cranberry juice and sorbet and blend until smooth.

Transfer to a shallow freezerproof container and freeze for 4 hours. Return to the blender and process to form a slushie.

LEFT TO RIGHT
frozen cranberry, raspberry & grapefruit slushie
guava, strawberry & apple refresher
mango & strawberry delight
(recipe on page 55)

Make your own version of this tropical smoothie depending on what's good in the market that day. Star fruit (carambola), lychees, melons of all sorts – all are good. Take care with colours though: red and green make an unappetizing grey.

tropical fruit smoothie
with pineapple, watermelon, strawberries & lime

2 limes

10 ice cubes

6 strawberries, hulled

1 small pineapple, peeled, cored and chopped

¼ watermelon, peeled and deseeded

your choice of other fruit such as: 6 canned lychees, drained and deseeded

2 bananas, peeled and sliced

1 custard apple, deseeded

berries such as raspberries or redcurrants

sugar, to taste (optional)

serves 4 6

Finely slice one of the limes and reserve. Grate the zest and squeeze the juice of the other.

Put the ice cubes in a blender and work to a snow. Add all the prepared fruit, in batches if necessary, and blend until smooth. Add the lime zest and juice and blend again. Add sugar, if preferred, then serve in chilled glasses with the slices of lime.

fruit juices
& coolers

Choose your favourite juices to make these granitas. You might prefer one variety, or several. Thick juices like pear, peach and apricot are especially good. Serve the ices straight after crushing – they melt fast.

frozen fruit juice granitas

1½ litres/6 cups fruit juice or purée of your choice, such as mango, cranberry or organic apple juice, or pear nectar

sugar, to taste

serves 4

Add sugar so that the juice is just a little sweeter than you like to drink it (freezing reduces sweetness). Fill ice cube trays with the fruit juice. Freeze.

When ready to serve, turn out into 4 small bowls and crush with a fork – you are aiming for an icy texture, not smooth like an ice cream. Serve in small glasses with spoons.

Fennel can be very difficult to juice – you need a strong machine. Alternatively, chop it and purée in a blender with apple juice, then strain. Use a crisp, sweet red apple such as Red Delicious to give a wonderful pinkish tinge. Always remember to remove the stem and stalk ends of apples and pears, as this is where any pesticides and residues collect.

apple juice with fennel

1 fennel bulb
2 apples, cored but not peeled
juice of ½ lemon (optional)

serves 1–2

Trim the feathery green leaves from the fennel bulb (reserve a few sprigs), trim off the root end, then slice the bulb into long wedges and cut out and remove the cores from each wedge. Cut the apples into wedges. Put the apples and fennel through a juicer.

Stir in the lemon juice to stop discoloration, then serve immediately, topped with the reserved fennel sprigs for extra scent.

This recipe is best made with cooking apples – they turn to delicious apple-flavoured foam when boiled. Cooked apple drinks are usually pale, but fresh juices made from red apples will be pink if you juice them with the skins on. For a much quicker result, use fresh apple juice, omit the sugar, add the fresh lemon juice and fill with sparkling mineral water.

apple lemonade

2–3 cooking apples, unpeeled, chopped into small pieces
sugar, to taste
freshly squeezed juice of 1 lemon
sparkling mineral water, to top up
ice cubes, to serve

serves 4

Put the apples in a saucepan, cover with cold water, bring to the boil and simmer until soft. Strain, pressing the pulp through the sieve/strainer with a spoon. Add sugar to taste, stir until dissolved, then leave to cool.

To serve, pack a jug/pitcher with ice, half-fill the glass with the apple juice, add the lemon juice and top up with sparkling mineral water.

Any apples will do, but unpeeled Granny Smiths produce the most beautiful green. The ginger is optional, but utterly delicious, and the mint leaves give an even brighter green. Lime juice will stop the apple juice turning brown so quickly, but drink this concoction immediately – don't let it hang around, or you lose all the benefits of freshly crushed juice.

minty ginger granny smith

4 Granny Smith apples, cored but not peeled, then cut into chunks

4–8 sprigs of fresh mint

a chunk of fresh ginger, peeled and sliced (optional)

1 tablespoon freshly squeezed lime juice (optional)

serves 1

Push half the apples through a juicer, then the mint, ginger and lime juice, if using. Finally, push through the remaining apples and serve.

variation: Frozen Apple Margarita
Put 250 ml/1 cup crushed ice in a blender, add the juice and blend to a froth. The Margarita is ready when the sound of the motor changes – that means the mixture has risen away from the blades.

Basil limeade is perfect to serve to guests at a brunch gathering. The amount of lime and sugar is a personal thing, so you adjust it to taste, adding more of one or the other as necessary. There will be guests who will appreciate a cheeky dash of cachaça rum in theirs for a caipirinha-style cocktail, but it is just as nice as a non-alcoholic refresher at any time of day.

basil limeade

225 ml/scant 1 cup freshly squeezed lime juice (from about 10 limes)
75 g/⅓ cup light muscovado/brown sugar
a handful of basil leaves (about 20 g/¾ oz.)
2 handfuls of ice cubes
250 ml/1 cup soda water

serves 4–6

Before you begin, place the glasses in the freezer to chill for one hour before use.

Put the lime juice, sugar and basil in a blender (one that is able to crush ice) and blend until smooth. Add the ice and blend briefly to break up the ice cubes. Pour into the chilled glasses and top up with the soda water.

Serving a glass of chilled homemade lemonade on a sweltering summer's day conjures up images of Edwardian house parties and Merchant Ivory films – all white muslin and cucumber sandwiches. But fresh lemonade is simple to make, and if you keep the lemony syrup in the refrigerator, you have an almost instant drink to dilute with either chilled sparkling mineral water or soda water.

homemade fresh lemonade

**thinly pared zest and
freshly squeezed juice of
6 large juicy lemons
175 g/1 cup sugar
sparkling mineral water or soda
water, chilled, to dilute**

to serve

**ice cubes
fresh lemon slices
sprigs of fresh mint**

serves 6–8

Put the lemon zest, sugar and 625 ml/2½ cups water in a non-aluminium saucepan and bring slowly to a simmer, stirring to dissolve the sugar. As soon as the sugar is dissolved and the syrup begins to bubble, take it off the heat. Half cover and leave until cold. Add the lemon juice to the cold syrup. Strain into a bowl or jug/pitcher, cover and chill.

Serve in a glass jug/pitcher with ice cubes, lemon slices and sprigs of mint, diluted with chilled sparkling mineral water or soda water on a ratio of about 1 part syrup to 1 part water.

variation
Add saffron to the lemonade to produce a startlingly golden-hued drink with an intriguing, refreshing taste. Just sprinkle a small pinch of saffron threads into the warm syrup when you take it off the heat.

This refreshing cooler is perfect if you are feeling overheated or need a quick pick-me-up. It is packed with vitamin C, one of the key nutrients that you need to boost your immune system.

citrus fizz

5 oranges, halved horizontally
1 red or pink grapefruit,
halved horizontally
½ lemon
2 large scoops of lemon sorbet
sparkling mineral water, chilled,
to top up

serves 2

Use a citrus press or hand-held juicer (reamer) to squeeze the juice from the oranges and grapefruit. Pour the juice through a sieve/strainer into 2 tall glasses and add a squeeze of juice from the lemon half to each one.

Add a large scoop of lemon sorbet to each glass and top up with chilled sparkling mineral water. Serve with a long-handled spoon.

All three fruits here are a valuable source of vitamin C, so this tangy juice is perfect for an early morning boost. Vitamin C aids against gum disease, helps protect our bodies from cancer, heart disease, colds and flu and reduces stress. It is even believed to delay the ageing process, as it promotes healthy skin. The white pith on citrus fruits is high in antioxidants, so include it in the juice for its health benefits.

vitamin C boost juice

6 oranges
3 ruby grapefruit
500 g/1 lb. 2 oz. strawberries
ice cubes, to serve

serves 3–4

Peel and chop the oranges and grapefruit, leaving some of the pith intact (see recipe introduction). Hull the strawberries and press all the fruit through a juicer into a pitcher/jug. Serve poured over ice.

Pussyfoot is one of the best non-alcoholic drinks, and greatly appreciated by designated drivers and pregnant women. Make sure the juices are freshly squeezed – bottled or carton juice just will not do. Leave out the egg yolk if you are pregnant or if there's any other risk involved – it won't matter greatly, and you can always add a tablespoon of cream instead.

pussyfoot

50 ml/¼ cup freshly squeezed orange juice

2 tablespoons freshly squeezed lemon juice

2 tablespoons freshly squeezed lime juice

1–2 tablespoons grenadine

1 free-range egg yolk (optional)

ice cubes

serves 1

Pour the orange, lemon and lime juices, grenadine and egg yolk, if using, into a cocktail shaker half-filled with ice cubes. Shake well and strain into a glass filled with more ice cubes.

variation
Add a dash of sparkling mineral water or lemonade for bit of festive fizz.

These summer fruits, now available all year round, make a delicious, refreshing drink. Juice them for breakfast to have instead of tea or coffee.

melon & strawberry juice

1 melon, such as cantaloupe or honeydew, deseeded and peeled

1 punnet/basket strawberries, about 250 g/2 cups, hulled

freshly squeezed juice of 2 limes

8 ice cubes, plus extra to serve

serves 4

Chop the melon flesh into small pieces and put in a blender with the strawberries, lime juice and ice. Blend until smooth and pour into a large chilled jug/pitcher. Serve over ice.

A pure, clean-tasting drink for a delicious and nutritious breakfast treat. Serve it ice cold for maximum refreshment.

super juice

1 pineapple or 400 g/14 oz. canned pineapple chunks in natural juice

3 large bananas, peeled and sliced

200 ml/scant 1 cup cranberry juice

8 ice cubes

serves 4

If using fresh pineapple, top and tail it, cut away the skin and remove all the dark prickly spots. Cut the pineapple into quarters lengthways, then remove the core from each section. Chop the fruit and put in a large jug/pitcher.

Add the bananas, cranberry juice and ice, then whizz with a hand-held blender until there are no lumps. Serve in chilled glasses.

LEFT *super juice*
RIGHT *melon & strawberry juice*

LEFT *cranberry cooler*
RIGHT *st. clement's*

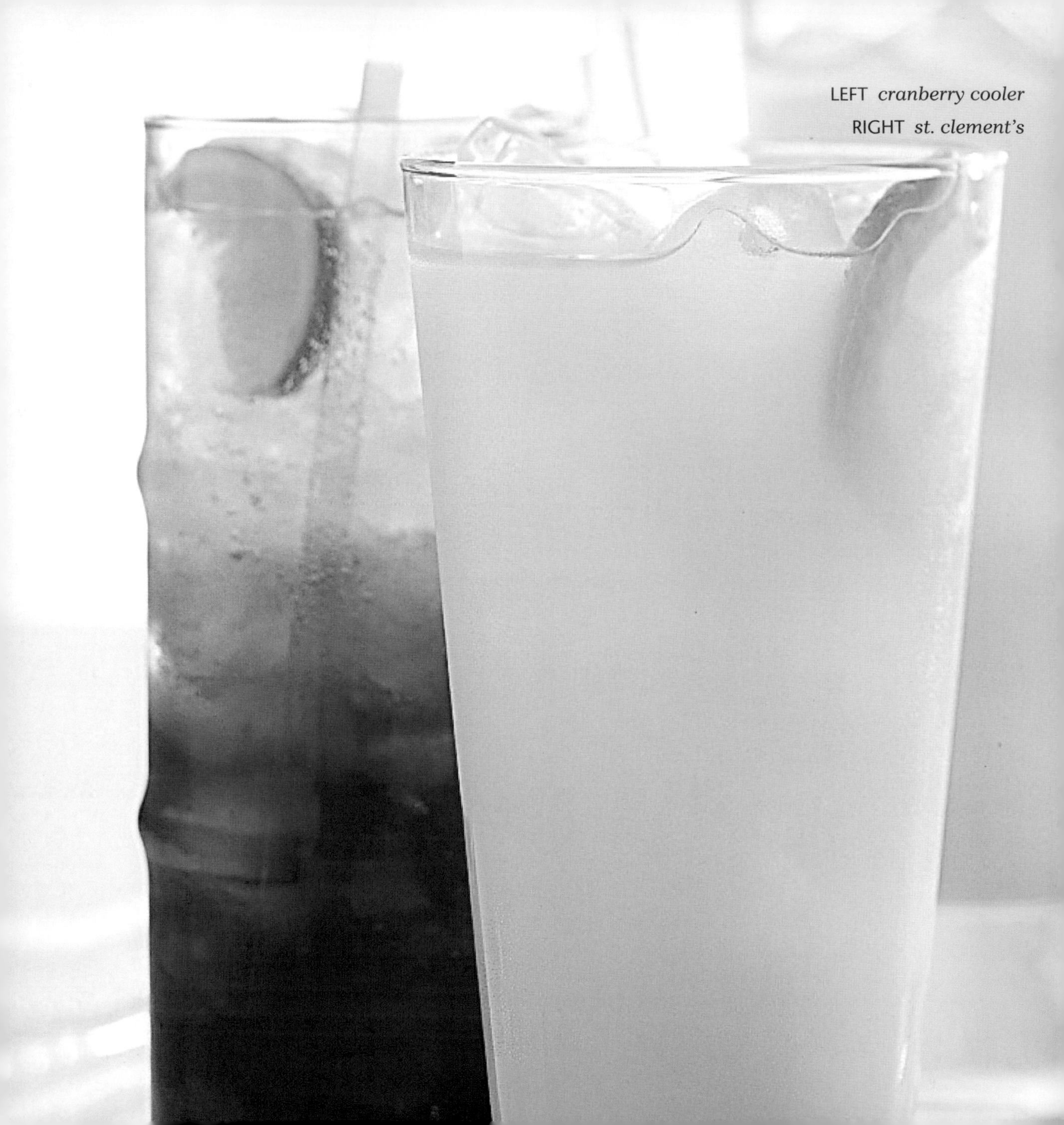

It's so simple: a Cranberry Cooler, when served ice cold and in the right proportions, is the only thing that almost beats a lemonade made just right!

cranberry cooler

250 ml/1 cup soda water
250 ml/1 cup cranberry juice
freshly squeezed lime juice, to taste
crushed ice, to serve

serves 2

Fill 2 tall glasses with crushed ice. Pour in equal parts of soda water and then cranberry juice. Add a squeeze or two of lime juice to taste and serve.

This refreshing, summery citrus drink takes its name from the English nursery rhyme 'Oranges and Lemons said the bells of St. Clement's'.

st. clement's

250 ml/1 cup bitter lemon
250 ml/1 cup freshly squeezed orange juice
lemon slices, to garnish
ice cubes, to serve

serves 2

Fill 2 tall glasses with ice cubes. Pour in equal parts of bitter lemon and orange juice. Stir gently, garnish each drink with a lemon slice and serve.

This non-alcoholic refresher is a play on the classic cranberry, grapefruit and vodka cocktail Sea Breeze (see page 226) but with the cranberry juice frozen into ice cubes. It's fun and funky at the same time.

sea freeze

300 ml/1¼ cups cranberry juice
400 ml/1⅔ cups fresh grapefruit juice
old-fashioned lemonade, to top up
lime slices, to garnish

serves 2

Pour the cranberry juice into a 12-hole ice cube tray and freeze for at least 4 hours.

Divide the cubes between 2 tall glasses and add the grapefruit juice. Top up with lemonade and garnish with a slice of lime to serve.

The berry ice cubes give this drink a pretty party feel. Make it in a large jug and let it sit for 10 minutes before serving – that way the ice cubes begin to melt, and the berry juices colour the drink a delicate pink.

elderflower & berry cup

150 g/1¼ cups mixed berries, such as raspberries, strawberries (hulled) and blueberries
125 ml/½ cup elderflower cordial
sparkling mineral water, to top up
elderflowers, to garnish (optional)

serves 4

Divide the berries between the ice cube tray holes and top up with still water. Freeze for 2 hours or until frozen.

Unmould the ice cubes into a large jug/pitcher or 4 tall glasses and pour in the elderflower cordial. Top up with sparkling water, garnish with a few elderflowers, if using, and serve.

Iced teas are a typical Louisiana-style refreshment. Served in tall, elegant glasses, iced tea is a drink that's well suited to the grand colonial homes prevalent in this part of the US. Fresh peaches or nectarines can be used instead of apricots, if preferred.

iced Louisiana apricot tea

4 orange pekoe tea bags
2 sprigs of fresh rosemary, plus extra to garnish
1 litre/4 cups just-boiled water
300 ml/1¼ cups apricot nectar
6 fresh apricots, halved, stoned and sliced
sparkling mineral water, to top up
ice cubes, to serve

serves 6

Put the tea bags and rosemary in a heatproof jug/pitcher and pour in the just-boiled water. Leave to steep for 10 minutes, then remove and discard the tea bags. Let cool, chill for 1 hour and then remove and discard the rosemary.

Stir in the apricot nectar, apricots and ice cubes and pour into tall glasses. Top up each drink with sparkling mineral water and garnish with a sprig of rosemary to serve.

This is a delicately flavoured iced tea, full of exotic flavours. If you are lucky enough to find fresh lychees you can use those and simply add a little honey for sweetness, otherwise canned lychees in a light syrup will work well too.

jasmine & lychee iced tea

1 tablespoon Jasmine tea leaves
1 litre/4 cups just-boiled water
2 star anise, bashed lightly
400 g/14 oz. can lychees in syrup, deseeded
clear sparkling lemonade, to top up

to serve
ice cubes
lime wedges
sprigs of fresh mint

serves 6

Put the tea leaves in a warmed teapot or heatproof jug/pitcher and pour in the just-boiled water. Leave to infuse for 5 minutes, then strain the tea into a clean jug/pitcher. Add the star anise and let cool.

Half-fill 6 tall glasses with ice and add 3 lychees and 2 tablespoons of the syrup to each one. Add a few lime wedges and mint sprigs to the glasses and top up with lemonade to serve.

jasmine & lychee iced tea

The four melon varieties used in this drink are all very aromatic. Some juicers produce a froth, but if yours is less muscular, you could layer the juices to form orange and green stripes. Wonderful for a summer brunch party. Melons have a delicate, elusive flavour and a delightful texture. Melon and ginger is one of the great food marriages, so a dash of ground ginger or fresh ginger juice is utterly wonderful.

melon froth

1–2 melons (orange cantaloupe or charentais, or green galia or honeydew), halved, deseeded and peeled
ginger syrup, to taste (optional)

serves 1–2

Put the melons through a juicer. Layer the colours in glasses if preferred, or serve separately. If using ginger syrup, serve it separately.

Melon and ginger are natural partners, and orange-fleshed melons are richer in vitamin C and beta-carotene than other varieties. Ginger is known for its anti-nausea benefits and people often find melon easier to manage than other fruits if they are feeling a bit queasy.

melon & ginger wake-up

2 cm/1 inch piece fresh ginger, peeled
1 cantaloupe melon, cut into thin wedges, deseeded and peeled

serves 2

Put the ginger and melon through a juicer, stir and pour the juice into 2 glasses.

variation
In place of the melon, substitute 1 small pineapple, halved, skin removed, cored and cut into wedges. Put through a juicer with the ginger and stir before serving.

You can select nectarines or peaches for this recipe, both of which add richness to the juice as well as providing a valuable vitamin C boost.

peach & orange nectar

5 ripe peaches or nectarines, halved, stoned and quartered
3 oranges, halved horizontally
ice cubes, to serve (optional)

serves 2

Put the peaches or nectarines through a juicer.

Use a citrus press or hand-held juicer (reamer) to squeeze the juice from the oranges. Stir together the peach or nectarine and orange juices, then pour into 2 glasses. Add ice, if liked.

peach & orange nectar

This utterly delicious juice combo is a great way to start the day – the ginger adds a surprising warm and lively note. Kiwi fruit contains large amounts of vitamin C, and you could add a little watercress or rocket for a green, peppery hit, if desired. Juices and smoothies taste much better if the fruit is only just ripe (or even a little underripe); if too ripe, the taste will be dull.

pear, apple & kiwi fruit juice
with fresh ginger

1 not-too-ripe pear
1 apple
2 not-too-ripe kiwi fruit
2.5 cm/1 inch piece fresh ginger,
peeled

serves 1

Peel and core the pear and apple and cut them into 6 wedges each. Peel and quarter the kiwi fruit. Put the pear through the juicer first, followed by the ginger, kiwi fruit and finally the apple. Stir well before serving, because it can separate. Drink as soon as possible and just feel those vitamins coursing through your body!

variation
Put all the prepared fruits and ginger in a blender with 150 ml/⅔ cup plain yoghurt. Blend until smooth, adding a squeeze of lemon juice or a little salt to taste

Commercially produced pear juice is delicious – but when freshly squeezed, especially over ice, it's out of this world. There also seems to be a particular affinity between pears and ginger. Pears must be eaten on the day they become ripe – left longer, their texture becomes 'sleepy'. Juicing is their saviour.

gingered pear juice

2–3 pears, quartered and cored
a chunk of fresh ginger, peeled
and sliced
ice cubes, to serve

serves 1

Put 1 pear through the juicer, then the ginger, then the remaining pear or pears. Serve immediately over ice.

LEFT *pomegranate & orange sunrise*
RIGHT *pineapple & mint agua fresca*

Refreshing *agua fresca* is found all over Mexico. The name literally means 'cold water' and it can be any fruit (or even another ingredient such as tamarind or rice and milk) blended with ice, sugar and water. The idea is that it is cooling and rehydrating on a hot day. Serve it as a fruit frappé just with ice, or as a sparkling drink mixed with soda water.

pineapple & mint agua fresca

100 g/½ cup granulated sugar
a smallish pineapple (about 700 g/
1 lb. 9 oz.), peeled and cored
a small handful of fresh mint leaves,
plus extra to serve
ice cubes, to serve
600 ml/2½ cups chilled soda water
(optional)

serves 4–8

Put the sugar and 100 ml/scant ½ cup water in a saucepan and heat gently until the sugar has dissolved. Remove from the heat and leave to cool while you cut the pineapple into rough chunks. Put the pineapple in a blender with the mint and the cooled syrup. Blend until smooth. Divide between 4 tumblers with a scoop of ice in each one, or 8 tall glasses, and top up with ice and the soda water.

A twist on the usual tequila sunrise, this drink is made with the now fashionable pomegranate juice, which adds a twist of bitterness to cut through the natural sweetness of orange juice. You can also add a shot of Campari to the pomegranate juice too, but this makes it an entirely different kind of morning!

pomegranate & orange sunrise

500 ml/2 cups freshly squeezed
orange juice
200 ml/scant 1 cup pure
pomegranate juice
ice cubes, to serve

serves 2

Half-fill 2 tumblers with ice and top up with orange juice so they are two-thirds full. Pour the pomegranate juice slowly down the side of the glass so it sinks to the bottom. Serve straightaway with a cocktail stirrer.

A summer cooler that's the most glorious colour and tastes like heaven! Strawberries in any guise please the palate and look wonderfully pretty. They're terrific with pineapple and sensational with rhubarb.

This unusual, old-fashioned drink is based on homemade lemonade. Make it with pretty pink forced rhubarb for an utterly stunning colour, or add a dash of grenadine to point up the pink.

pineapple & strawberry crush

1 pineapple, peeled and cored

10–12 ripe strawberries, hulled

grated zest and freshly squeezed juice of 2 lemons

2 tablespoons icing/confectioners' sugar, or to taste

freshly squeezed juice of 2 oranges

to serve

ice cubes or crushed ice

3–6 strawberries, hulled and sliced

a twist of orange, lime or lemon zest

serves 6–8

Put the pineapple, strawberries, lemon zest and icing/confectioners' sugar in a blender, add about 125 ml/½ cup iced water and purée until smooth. Add the orange and lemon juices and another 125 ml/½ cup iced water. Taste and add extra sugar if necessary (depending on the sweetness of the fruit). Pour into a jug/pitcher of ice and decorate with sliced strawberries and a twist of orange, lime or lemon zest.

rhubarb strawberryade

500 g/1 lb. 2 oz. rhubarb, trimmed and sliced

2 tablespoons icing/confectioners' sugar

grated zest and freshly squeezed juice of 1 lemon

1 litre/4 cups boiling water, or to cover

6 strawberries, hulled and halved

sparkling mineral water, to top up

ice cubes or crushed ice, to serve

serves 4–8

Put the rhubarb, sugar and lemon zest into a saucepan and cover with the boiling water. Stew until the rhubarb is very soft. Add the strawberries and boil hard for about 1 minute, then strain into a jug/pitcher, cool and chill. To serve, pour into a jug/pitcher of ice, stir in the lemon juice and top up with sparkling mineral water.

rhubarb strawberryade

Sweet and delicious, fresh pineapple also contains the enzyme bromelian, which helps with digestion. It is soothing for sore throats, coughs and upset stomachs.

pineapple crush

1 large pineapple, peeled and cored
freshly squeezed juice of 1 lemon
4 passion fruit (optional)
sugar or honey, to taste (optional)
ice cubes, to serve

serves 4

Cut the pineapple into wedges, then chunks and press through a juicer. Add the lemon juice and pour the mixture into a jug/pitcher of ice. Stir in the flesh and seeds of 3 passion fruit, if using, and top with the remaining flesh and seeds. Depending on the sweetness and ripeness of the pineapple, you may like to add a little sugar or honey.

Pomegranates have an intriguing sweet-tart flavour and a colour straight out of the Arabian Nights. In the Middle East and Pakistan, the fruit are the size of grapefruit and a deep purple-red, with juice to match. Their taste is very refreshing in hot weather. Mix them with orange juice for a slightly sweeter drink, and don't press the seeds too hard, or bitter flavours will be released.

pomegranate squeeze

3 pomegranates
1 orange (optional)
1 tablespoon grenadine (optional)
ice cubes, to serve

serves 1

Cut the pomegranates and orange, if using, in half horizontally. Using a citrus press or hand-held juicer (reamer), squeeze the juice from the pomegranates and orange. Add the grenadine, if using, then serve over ice.

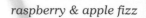
raspberry & apple fizz

This is a truly refreshing drink for a hot summer's day, and with the addition of the sparkling water it makes a delightful non-alcoholic cocktail.

raspberry & apple fizz

300 g/2¼ cups frozen raspberries
250 ml/1 cup apple juice
12 ice cubes
sparkling mineral water, to top up

serves 4

Put the raspberries, apple juice and ice in a blender and blend until smooth. Pour into 4 tall glasses and top up with sparkling mineral water.

A perfectly ripe mango is aromatic, with an ambrosial flavour and creamy-smooth silky texture. Combined with raspberries and a cranberry juice base, mango makes a perfect replenishing energy drink after strenuous exercise.

mango, raspberry & cranberry cruise

1 large mango, about 550 g/1 lb. 4 oz.
150 g/1¼ cups frozen raspberries
250 ml/1 cup cranberry juice
1 teaspoon honey (optional)

serves 2

Slice down each side of the mango stone and cut away the flesh from the skin. Put the flesh in a blender, add the raspberries and cranberry juice and blend until smooth. Taste and add the honey to sweeten, if necessary.

Making your own cordials or fruit syrups is so satisfying as with very little effort you have a delicious fruit drink mixer that will last you for ages. You could use other berries, such as blackberries or raspberries, and top up with still or sparkling mineral water or clear lemonade.

blueberry cordial with apple fizz

300 g/2¼ cups frozen blueberries
300 g/1½ cups sugar
sparkling apple juice, to top up
ice cubes, to serve

makes 500 ml/2 cups cordial

Place the blueberries and sugar in a large saucepan and heat gently until the blueberries soften and the sugar dissolves. Bring to the boil and simmer over a medium heat for 15 minutes, until syrupy.

Strain through a fine sieve/strainer and pour into a sterilized bottle (see note on page 4). Seal and leave to cool.

To serve, pour 2–3 tablespoons of cordial into tall glasses, add a few ice cubes and top up with sparkling apple juice. The cordial will keep in the refrigerator for 4 weeks.

LEFT *chilled lemongrass tisane*
RIGHT *orange & apple refresher*

Tisane is the French word for an infusion of herbs, flowers or other aromatics – it's a beautiful word for this deliciously spicy drink, which is chilled down to make a great contrast between hot and cold.

chilled lemongrass tisane

1–2 red chillies, deseeded and sliced

2–4 lemongrass stalks, outer leaves discarded, inner section finely sliced

5 cm/2 inch piece fresh ginger, peeled and sliced

50 g/¼ cup sugar

1 litre/4 cups boiling water

freshly squeezed juice of 2 lemons

fresh mint leaves, to serve

ice cubes, to serve

serves 4

Put the chilli into a heatproof jug/pitcher with the lemongrass, ginger and sugar, then add the boiling water and the lemon juice and stir to dissolve the sugar. Leave to infuse until cold.

Strain the cooled liquid and chill for at least 30 minutes. Serve in tall glasses with mint leaves and ice cubes.

Some juicers have a citrus attachment as well as a juicer, so this drink couldn't be simpler. If you don't have the citrus press, just peel the oranges and put them through the regular juicer (don't forget to remove all the bitter white pith).

orange & apple refresher

2 large oranges, peeled

2 Granny Smith apples

2.5 cm/1 inch fresh ginger, peeled

ice cubes, to serve

serves 2

Push the oranges, apples and the ginger through a juicer. Half-fill 2 tall glasses with ice cubes, pour the juice over the top and serve.

Strawberries with balsamic vinegar – it sounds a rather odd combination, but balsamic acts like lemon juice, to point up other flavours, and its sweet, spicy undertones have an extraordinarily delicious effect. Balsamic – the rich, slightly sweet, aged vinegar from Italy – should be used in moderation. Use it like a spice; don't slap it on like ordinary vinegar. It also has a special affinity with strawberries.

strawberry juice with balsamic

2 punnets/baskets ripe strawberries, about 250 g/2 cups, hulled
1 tablespoon honey (optional)
6 ice cubes, plus extra to serve
balsamic vinegar, to serve

serves 2–4

Reserve a few strawberries for decoration, then put the remainder in a blender with the honey, if using, and the ice cubes. Blend well, adding water if necessary to make the mixture easier to work. Blend again, then serve in a tiny shot glass, over ice, with a reserved halved strawberry on top. Serve the balsamic separately, to add in drops.

watermelon kick

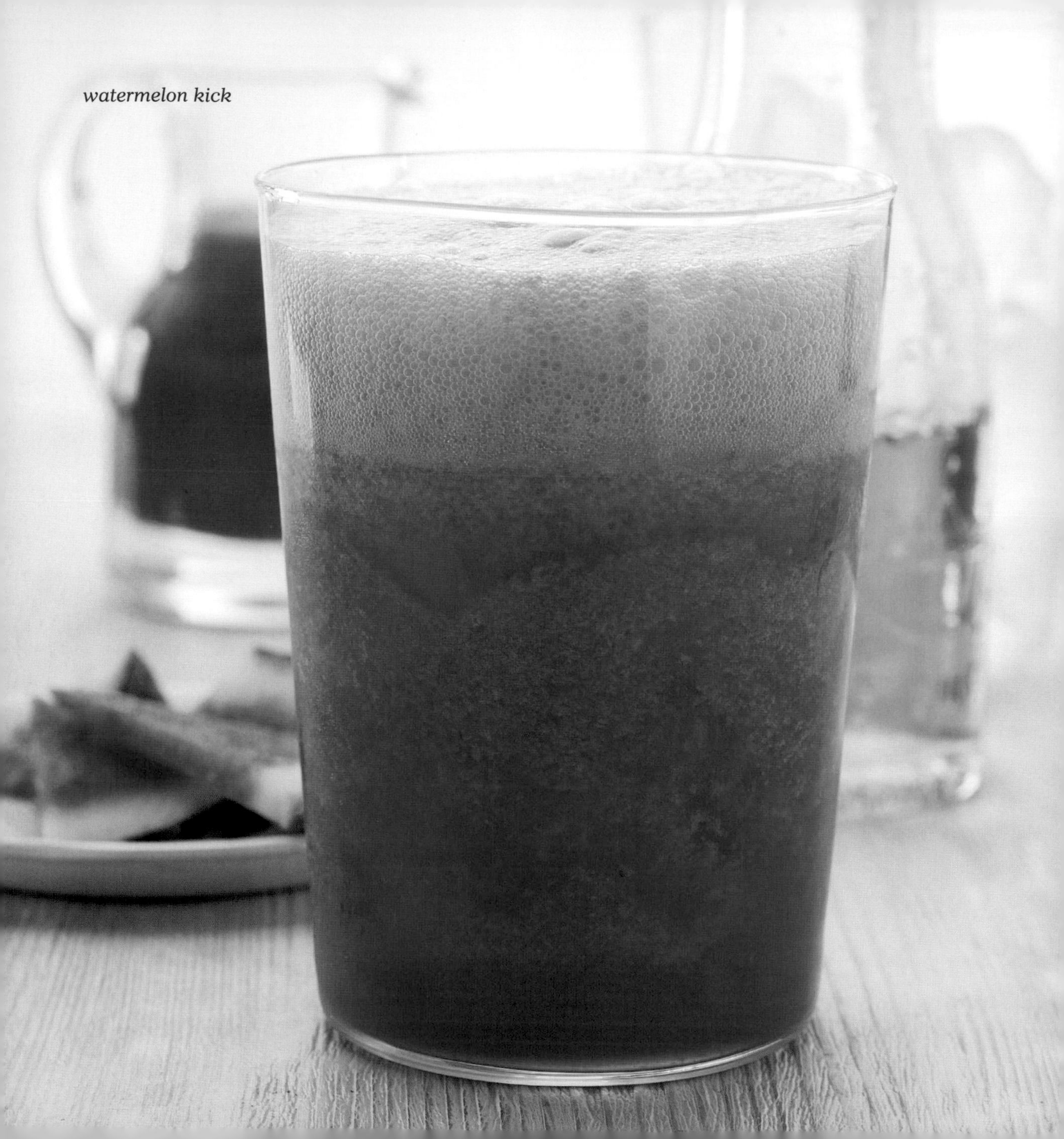

Watermelons are super tasty and sweet, and are great thrist-quenchers. This refreshing drink is perfect for rehydration on a hot summer's day, the season they are at their very best. It is also a rich source of vitamins C and A.

watermelon kick

200 g/7 oz. watermelon, peeled, deseeded and diced
2 tablespoons lime cordial
100 ml/scant ½ cup freshly squeezed pink grapefruit juice
tonic water, to top up
ice cubes, to serve

serves 2

Put the watermelon and lime cordial in a blender or liquidizer and whizz until smooth.

Put a few ice cubes into 2 tall glasses and add half the watermelon mixture and half the grapefruit juice to each glass. Top up with tonic water and serve.

Indian and Moroccan sharbats are distantly related to the sherbets that are familiar to Westerners. If you have a juicer, use it to make watermelon juice. You can use a blender but it will give you a thicker consistency. You can buy ginger purée in supermarkets or make your own (see page 215).

watermelon & ginger sharbat

1 small, ripe watermelon, chilled
2 tablespoons ginger purée, or to taste
sugar, to taste
crushed ice, to serve

serves 2–4

Cut the watermelon in half, then remove and discard the seeds. Put the watermelon flesh and ginger into a blender and blend until smooth. Add water if the mixture is too thick. Taste and add sugar if needed, then serve over crushed ice.

In India, a typical summertime drink is the juice of a fresh lime, topped up with soda water. This recipe freezes the lime juice first so it melts into the soda.

Indian fresh frozen lime with soda

freshly squeezed juice of 6 large
limes, and shredded zest of 1 lime
(optional)
sugar, to taste
soda water, to top up

serves 4

Mix the lime juice with an equal amount of water and stir in sugar to taste. Pour into ice cube trays and freeze.

When ready to serve, divide the ice cubes into 4 glasses and top up with soda water. Add the shredded lime zest if preferred.

Watermelon makes a delicious drink and it is terrific with hot, spicy partners like ginger or even chilli. The lime zest and juice point up the flavour.

frozen watermelon, ginger & lime

1 ripe, round watermelon, halved and
deseeded
5 cm/2 inch piece fresh ginger,
peeled and grated
freshly squeezed juice of 2 limes
sugar, to taste (optional)
ice cubes, to serve

serves 4

Put the flesh of half the watermelon in a blender, add the ginger and lime juice and blend until smooth, adding water if necessary. Taste, stir in sugar if using, pour into ice cube trays and freeze. When ready to serve, put the remaining watermelon in the blender and blend until smooth. Divide the ice cubes between 4 glasses, top with the watermelon juice and serve.

LEFT *Indian fresh frozen lime with soda*
RIGHT *frozen watermelon, ginger & lime*

dairy smoothies & shakes

Cherries and chocolate are a marriage made in heaven. When cherries are in season, stone them and stuff the cavity with a candy-coated chocolate button (such as Smarties® or M&M's®). Freeze and use straightaway with chocolate ice cream and a smoothie made of stoned cherries – or keep them for later in the year, when you need to remind yourself of the taste of summer.

cherry-chocolate smoothie
with frozen cherries stuffed with smarties®

12 candy-coated chocolate buttons, such as Smarties® or M&M's®

36 cherries, stoned

12 ice cubes

iced water or milk (optional)

12 small scoops chocolate ice cream

serves 4

Press a Smartie® or M&M® into the cavities of 12 of the cherries. Open-freeze on a tray in the freezer.

When ready to serve, put the remaining stoned cherries in a blender, add the ice cubes and work to a purée, adding a little iced water or milk, if necessary, to help the machine run. Make the mixture as thick or thin as you prefer by adding more water or milk.

Put 3 scoops of chocolate ice cream in each of 4 tall glasses and pour over the puréed cherries. Top with the frozen stuffed cherries, then serve.

A luxurious steamed milk drink without the caffeine kick. If you have a coffee maker, use its steam element to foam the chocolate milk for a really frothy, almost cappuccino-like effect.

white chocolate frothy

600 ml/2½ cups organic milk
50 g/1¾ oz. white chocolate, grated
sweetened cocoa powder,
for sprinkling (optional)
ground cinnamon, for sprinkling
(optional)

serves 2

Warm 2 mugs or heatproof glasses. Heat the milk in a saucepan until it just reaches boiling point and then stir in the chocolate until melted. Froth the milk using a whisk, hand-held blender or coffee maker, and pour into the warmed mugs or glasses. Serve dusted with cocoa powder and ground cinnamon, if preferred.

Very thick, rich and totally divine, this drink is simply delicious. Coffee and chocolate are perfect partners – earthy, aromatic and satisfying. Use an organic, freshly roasted and ground coffee for an intense flavour and extra kick.

mocha ice cream special

500 ml/2 cups freshly brewed coffee
50 g/1¾ oz. dark chocolate, finely chopped
250 ml/1 cup organic milk
4 scoops vanilla ice cream
4 scoops chocolate ice cream

serves 2

As soon as the coffee is made, transfer it to a jug/pitcher and stir in the chocolate until melted. Set aside to cool.

Put the cold coffee in a blender with the milk and a scoop of each flavour of ice cream. Blend until smooth. Add a scoop each of vanilla and chocolate ice cream to 2 tall glasses, pour over the drink and serve.

LEFT *white chocolate frothy*
RIGHT *mocha ice cream special*

Milo powder is a chocolate-flavoured food supplement drink, available from supermarkets. It makes great shakes and other drinks. It contains essential minerals and vitamins and has a low glycaemic index. If you can't find Milo, use sweetened chocolate powder instead.

malted milo shake

2 tablespoons Milo (chocolate malt) powder, plus extra for sprinkling
600 ml/2½ cups organic milk
4 scoops vanilla ice cream

serves 2–3

Put all the ingredients in a blender and blend until smooth. Pour into glasses and serve sprinkled with extra Milo powder.

Lassi is the famous Indian drink made with yoghurt and ice, thinned down with a little water. It is served either salty or sweet, flavoured with fruit, nuts or spices. It is very cool and refreshing on a hot summer's day. Strawberries, mangoes, papayas or bananas are perfect fruits to team up with milk and yoghurt.

fruit salad lassi with strawberries

250 ml/1 cup low-fat yoghurt

125 ml/½ cup low-fat milk

6 large strawberries, hulled and halved

a choice of other fruit, such as 1 small punnet/basket raspberries, 6 apricots or 2 peaches, stoned

sugar, to taste

crushed ice, to serve

serves 2–4

Put the yoghurt, milk, strawberries and other fruit in a blender and process until creamy. Add sugar to taste and serve poured over crushed ice.

variation
Instead of the fruit listed, use the pulp and seeds of 4 passion fruit, plus 1 tablespoon Galliano or Grand Marnier liqueur.

apricot ice cream smoothie with cream

Apricots, like peaches and nectarines, are too dense to squeeze for juice – you have to purée them in a blender. The ice cream makes the mixture even more indulgent. Leave the skins on and they chop up into little pieces and give pretty colour and interesting texture.

apricot ice cream smoothie with cream

3 ice cubes

2 3 ripe apricots, halved, stoned and sliced

2 scoops vanilla or strawberry ice cream

1 small carton or can apricot nectar

milk or water

2 tablespoons cream or yoghurt, to serve (optional)

serves 1

Put the ice cubes in a blender and blend to a snow. Add the apricot slices, ice cream and apricot nectar. Blend until frothing and creamy, adding enough milk or water to make the blades run.

Put the mixture in a glass, swirl in the cream or yoghurt, if using, and serve with a spoon.

Roasting the peaches adds a sweet, caramel flavour to this drink and is a great idea if the peaches are slightly underripe. Orange-fleshed, freestone peaches are the best variety for colour and convenience, as the stones are easier to remove than those of clingstone varieties, but any type of peach will work.

roasted peaches & cream

2 peaches

1 teaspoon soft brown sugar

250 ml/1 cup organic milk

2 scoops vanilla ice cream

serves 2

Preheat the oven to 190°C/375°F/Gas 5. Cut the peaches in half and discard the stones. Arrange the peach halves cut side up in a foil-lined roasting tin and sprinkle over the sugar. Bake for 20–25 minutes until the peaches are tender, remove from the oven and set aside until cold.

Chop the peaches, transfer to a blender, add the remaining ingredients and blend until smooth.

This is a wholesome breakfast in a glass. Bananas add bulk as well as providing us with energy, oat bran helps reduce cholesterol levels and raisins are an antioxidant-rich fruit and instant energy source. The nutmeg adds a touch of spice and aids digestion and appetite.

banana, nutmeg & honey smoothie

2 bananas

1 teaspoon honey

2 tablespoons oat bran

2 tablespoons raisins

250 ml/1 cup organic skimmed milk

250 ml/1 cup organic low-fat yoghurt

**¼ teaspoon freshly grated nutmeg,
plus extra to dust**

serves 2

Peel the bananas and chop the flesh. Put it in a blender with the remaining ingredients and blend until smooth. Serve the smoothie dusted with a little extra grated nutmeg.

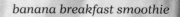

A filling breakfast – full of flavour, packed with calcium and fibre and very good for you! If you like your drinks less sweet, reduce the quantity of honey. You can also substitute other fruit in season, such as berries, which should be chilled when used in smoothies.

banana breakfast smoothie

250 ml/1 cup low-fat milk

250 ml/1 cup low-fat yoghurt

2 tablespoons crushed ice

1 tablespoon honey

1 banana, peeled and chopped

1 tablespoon wheatgerm

serves 2–4

Put all the ingredients in a blender and blend until smooth. Add extra fruit if preferred.

This is another energy drink best consumed before aerobic activity. Bananas provide an instant and sustained energy boost, which is why we often see sports people eating them during a game. In fact, just two bananas will provide the body with enough energy for a 90-minute workout!

bananarama

2 large bananas

300 ml/1¼ cups buttermilk

1 tablespoon honey

serves 2

Peel and chop the bananas and put in a blender with the buttermilk and honey. Blend until smooth

pictured on page 38

Protein-rich milk and almonds combine to provide beneficial amounts of the antioxidant vitamin E, B vitamins and healthy oils and minerals, including bone-building calcium. The almonds also add a wonderful creaminess.

almond & banana shake

65 g/½ cup whole blanched almonds

400 ml/1⅔ cups semi-skimmed milk

2 ripe bananas, peeled and thickly sliced

1 teaspoon vanilla extract

freshly grated nutmeg, to serve

serves 2

Put the almonds in a food processor or blender and process until finely ground.

Add the milk, bananas and vanilla extract, then blend until smooth and creamy. Pour into 2 glasses and sprinkle a little nutmeg over the top.

Satisfying and filling, this smoothie is full of vital nutrients and energy to kick-start your day. The milk and yoghurt provide calcium, protein and B vitamins, while the fruit serves up vitamin C and magnesium, both essential for healthy bones and teeth.

strawberry & banana smoothie

2 bananas, peeled and sliced

250 g/2 cups strawberries, hulled

½ teaspoon vanilla extract (optional)

150 ml/⅔ cup thick, natural low-fat bio yoghurt

350 ml/1½ cups semi-skimmed milk

serves 2

Put all the ingredients in a blender and blend until the mixture is thick, smooth and creamy. Pour the smoothie into 2 glasses and serve.

LEFT *almond & banana shake*
RIGHT *strawberry & banana smoothie*

LEFT *coconut banana shake*
RIGHT *coconut milk with mango*

Coconut milk and bananas are a traditional Thai combination – add a dash of dark rum as an optional extra. The result is a Thailand-meets-the-Caribbean mixture! The mango variation can be made with fresh mango, or canned Alphonso mango puree (see page 150).

coconut banana shake

about 250 ml/1 cup canned coconut milk

250 ml/1 cup low-fat milk

2 ripe bananas, peeled and chopped

1 tablespoon dark rum, or to taste (optional)

sugar, to taste

crushed ice, to serve

serves 1–2

Place all the ingredients except the sugar and ice in a blender. Whizz, adding sugar and more rum, to taste. Pour over crushed ice and serve.

variation: Coconut Milk with Mango
Use 250 ml/1 cup Alphonso mango purée or 1 large ripe fresh mango instead of the bananas and rum. Whizz until frothy and serve with a scoop of mango ice cream.

Kids will love this shake, particularly with a spoonful of extra ice cream. It's optional but recommended for a real treat!

chocolate & banana cinnamon shake

2 bananas

4 scoops chocolate ice cream, plus extra to serve (optional)

300 ml/1¼ cups milk

1 teaspoon ground cinnamon

serves 4

Peel and chop the bananas. Put the ice cream, bananas, milk and cinnamon in a blender and blend until smooth. Pour into 4 tall glasses and serve with an extra scoop of chocolate ice cream, if using.

Bananas make very good smoothies – add them to almost anything else and they will reward you with a sweet creaminess. Bananas have a special affinity with nuts – so peanut butter is gorgeous.

banana & peanut butter smoothie

2 large, ripe bananas

10 ice cubes

1 tablespoon sugar or sugar syrup, or to taste

125 ml/½ cup milk, yoghurt or single/light cream

4 tablespoons peanut butter

serves 1

Peel and cut the bananas into chunks. Put them in a blender with the remaining ingredients. Work to a purée. Thin with a little more milk or water if too thick, then serve.

banana & peanut butter smoothie

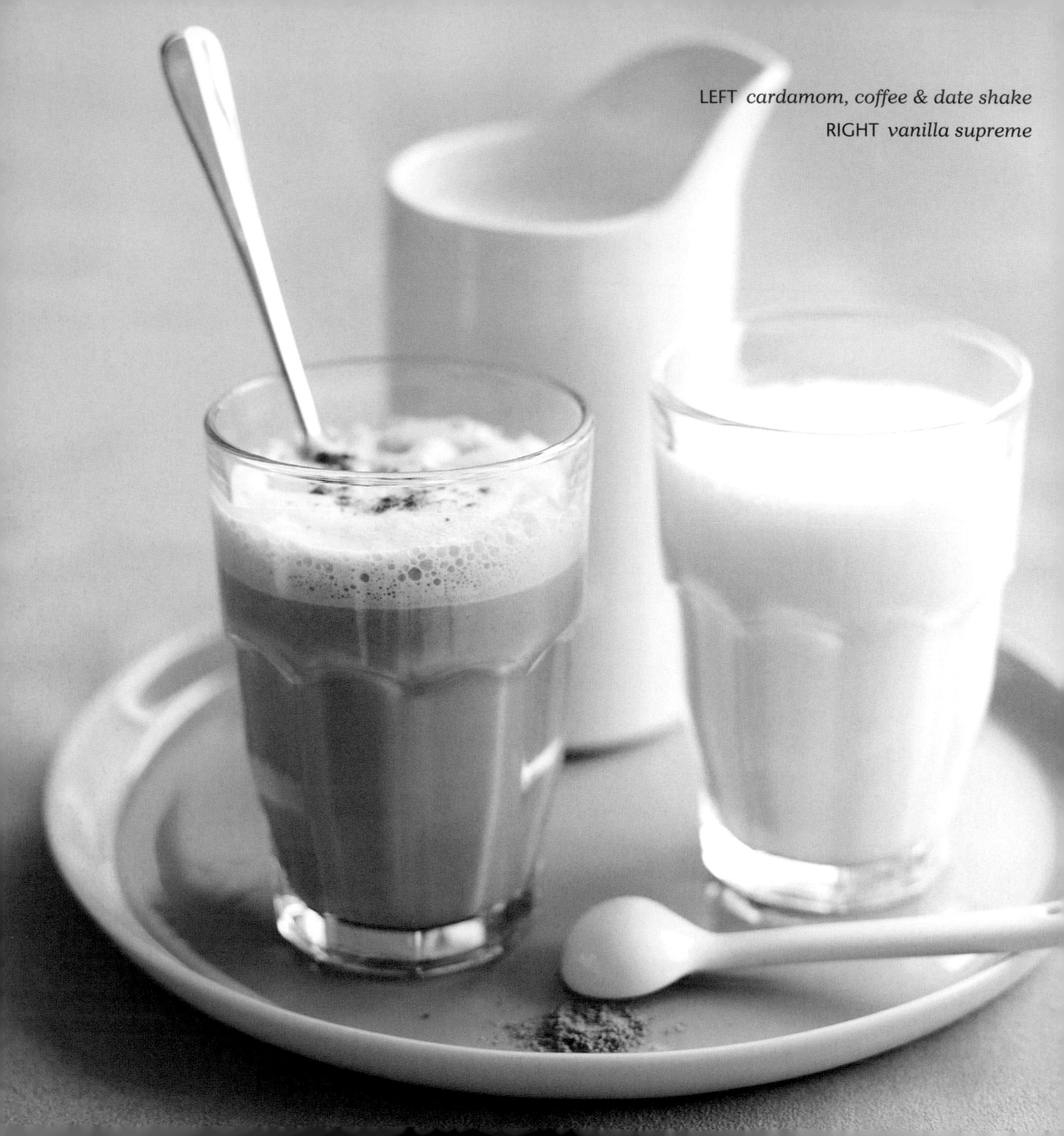

LEFT *cardamom, coffee & date shake*
RIGHT *vanilla supreme*

The addition of dates and ground cardamom gives this iced coffee drink a definite Middle Eastern flavour – a real hint of the exotic. Cardamom improves digestion and provides a heady aroma known to act as an aphrodisiac. Dates and coffee create energy and enhance vitality and libido when combined, so perhaps this is the perfect drink for lovers!

Vanilla adds a smooth texture to the milk and is reminiscent of old-fashioned milkshakes. The spice is also naturally mood-enhancing.

cardamom, coffee & date shake

4 Medjool dates, stoned

300 ml/1¼ cups organic milk

125 ml/½ cup cold espresso coffee

2 scoops vanilla ice cream

½–1 teaspoon ground cardamom, plus extra for sprinkling

serves 3

Put the dates in a saucepan with half the milk and heat very gently until the milk just reaches boiling point. Remove the pan from the heat and let cool completely. When cold, transfer the dates and milk to a blender and add the remaining milk, cold coffee, ice cream and cardamom. Blend until smooth. Pour into glasses and serve sprinkled with extra ground cardamom.

vanilla supreme

1 vanilla pod

4 scoops vanilla ice cream or sorbet

500 ml/2 cups organic milk

serves 2

Cut the vanilla pod in half lengthways and scrape the seeds into a blender. Add the ice cream and milk and blend until smooth.

In India, lassis are flavoured with rosewater, saffron, pistachio nuts or spices such as cardamom. Vanilla and chocolate flavours are more familiar to Western tastes, but you could also experiment and create your own.

vanilla or chocolate yoghurt lassi

300 ml/1¼ cups plain low-fat yoghurt
300 ml/1¼ cups skimmed milk
250 ml/1 cup crushed ice (optional)
a choice of:
2 tablespoons chocolate syrup,
or a few drops of vanilla extract,
or 1 teaspoon each of rosewater and crushed cardamom seeds
1 tablespoon sugar, or to taste (optional)

serves 1–2

Place the yoghurt, milk and crushed ice, if using, in a blender or food processor and whizz. Add the chosen flavouring and whizz again. Taste and add sugar if preferred.

Chai is a fragrant spiced milky tea from India. This smooth drink uses some of the same spices that feature in the tea, such as cardamom and cinnamon. Vanilla and a little sugar add sweetness.

chai vanilla milkshake

1 litre/4 cups full-fat milk
75 g/⅓ cup light muscovado/brown sugar
2 tablespoons black tea leaves
1 vanilla pod, split lengthways
¼ teaspoon ground cinnamon
8 cardamom pods
¼ teaspoon ground allspice
3 scoops vanilla ice cream

serves 4

Put 800 ml/3¼ cups of the milk, the sugar, tea leaves, vanilla pod, cinnamon, cardamom and allspice in a saucepan and bring to the boil. Reduce the heat and simmer gently for 5 minutes, then turn off the heat, cover and leave for 10 minutes. Strain into ice cube trays and freeze until solid. When ready to serve, put the frozen chai cubes in a blender or liquidizer with the remaining milk and the ice cream and whizz until smooth. Serve immediately.

chai vanilla milkshake

Freeze a selection of fresh juices in an ice cube tray and serve with buttermilk for breakfast. These ice cubes have been made with cranberry juice and strawberry purée. Ice cubes made from fruit juice melt more slowly than ordinary cubes, so you can top it up with more buttermilk or mineral water for a long, cool, delicious and filling drink.

berry ice blocks
with buttermilk froth

1 tray of ice cubes made with fruit juices

500 ml/2 cups buttermilk or low-fat yoghurt

sparkling mineral water or soda water, to top up (optional)

honey, to taste

serves 4

Fill 4 glasses with the fruity ice cubes, add a dollop of buttermilk or yoghurt, then top up with sparkling mineral water or soda water, if using. Serve honey separately and add to taste.

This smoothie can be made using either vanilla or chocolate ice cream. Although using vanilla preserves the vibrant blue-pink colour, blueberries are a great match for chocolate, especially chocolate ice cream, so it is a combination worth trying.

blueberry ice cream smoothie

1 punnet/basket blueberries, about 200 g/1⅔ cups, chilled

2 scoops ice cream, chocolate or vanilla

about 125 ml/½ cup low-fat milk, chilled

fresh mint leaves, to garnish (optional)

serves 1

Reserve a few blueberries to serve, then put the remainder in a blender. Add the ice cream and enough milk to make the blades run. Blend to a purée, then add extra milk to taste (the less you add, the thicker the smoothie will be). Pour the mixture into a glass and top with the reserved blueberries and mint leaves, if using.

This smoothie is a meal in a glass; it is easy to digest and perfect for a busy morning when you need breakfast on the run. To enhance absorption of the nutrients, chew the liquid to stimulate the production of saliva and digestive enzymes.

blueberry muesli smoothie

250 g/2 cups fresh or frozen blueberries
250 ml/1 cup organic yoghurt
250 ml/1 cup organic milk
50 g/⅓ cup muesli
1 teaspoon vanilla extract

serves 2

Put all the ingredients in a blender and then blend until smooth.

If you're a ginger fan, this recipe will be your idea of heaven. Another treat for ginger fiends is what is sometimes, intriguingly, called a 'Ginger Spider'. Place a big scoop of ice cream in a soda glass and top up with ginger ale.

ginger shake

6 pieces preserved ginger, in syrup, plus extra, chopped, to serve

100 ml milk/scant ½ cup, or to taste

3 scoops ice cream, plus extra to serve

sugar, to taste

serves 1–2

Place the ginger pieces, milk, ice cream and 6 tablespoons of the syrup in a blender, then purée to a froth. Taste and add extra milk and sugar if preferred. Serve topped with another small scoop of ice cream or some extra ginger, chopped.

Usually, fresh produce is far better than canned. However, if you can find canned Alphonso mango in an Asian market, buy it and try it in this recipe. The Alphonso is famously the greatest mango in the world! Otherwise, use very ripe fresh mango.

mango & ginger lassi
with low-fat yoghurt

250 ml/1 cup mango purée, fresh or canned

6 ice cubes

2.5 cm/1 inch piece fresh ginger, peeled and grated

250 ml/1 cup low-fat yoghurt

mineral water, ginger ale or semi-skimmed milk

sugar or honey, to taste (optional)

4 tablespoons diced fresh mango, to serve (optional)

serves 4

Put all the ingredients except the diced mango in a blender and work to a froth. Serve immediately, topped with the diced mango, if using.

*mango & ginger lassi
with low-fat yoghurt*

This recipe is based on the Pavlova – the national dessert of Australia and New Zealand, named in honour of the great Russian ballerina. The Pavlova consists of a large meringue, topped with fresh fruit and whipped cream. The fruit topping can be changed according to which fruits are in season, but almost always includes passion fruit, and is a particular treat for someone with a sweet tooth.

passion fruit meringue smoothie

2 small white meringues, about 5 cm/2 inches in diameter, plus 1 extra, crumbled, to serve (optional)

250 g/2 cups strawberries (or other fruit in season)

2 passion fruit, plus 1 extra, to serve (optional)

3 scoops ice cream, or to taste

100 ml milk/scant 1 cup, or to taste

1 tablespoon whipped cream, to serve (optional)

serves 1–2

Place the meringues, strawberries and milk in a blender or food processor, then whizz. Add the ice cream and the pulp and seeds of 2 passion fruit. Blend again. Taste and add extra milk if you like a thinner drink, or extra ice cream if you like it thicker. Pour into tall glasses and serve topped with the crumbled meringue, passion fruit pulp and whipped cream, if using.

To save a few minutes you can simply blend all the ingredients in one go, but the rippled effect achieved by swirling the peach and raspberry flavours together just before serving is very pretty. Both taste equally good.

peach melba ripple

4 canned peach halves in natural juice, drained

1 teaspoon vanilla extract

500 ml/2 cups organic milk

4 scoops vanilla ice cream

125 g/1 cup raspberries

serves 2–3

Put the peach halves, half the vanilla extract, half the milk and 2 scoops of vanilla ice cream in a blender. Blend until smooth and divide between 2 or 3 tumblers. Repeat with the raspberries and remaining vanilla, milk and ice cream. Drizzle the raspberry mixture carefully into the glasses to give a ripple effect.

Sharp and tangy, this rich confection is just like cheesecake in a glass. If you serve it with digestive biscuits/graham crackers or ginger biscuits for dipping, you almost have the real thing!

lemon cheesecake shake

100 g/3½ oz. cream cheese

grated zest and freshly squeezed juice of ½ unwaxed lemon

4 tablespoons lemon curd

125 ml/½ cup Greek yoghurt

250 ml/1 cup organic milk

serves 3–4

Put all the ingredients in a blender and blend until smooth.

LEFT *peach melba ripple*
RIGHT *lemon cheesecake shake*

Almond and rosewater make an aromatic and exotic drink – very refreshing on a hot summer's day served over ice. Magnesium and other minerals are found in almonds, and the combination of almonds and rosewater – a stress-reliever – in this lassi aids in calming the nerves and muscles.

almond lassi

50 g/½ cup whole blanched almonds
1 tablespoon rosewater
2 teaspoons soft brown sugar
300 ml/1¼ cups organic yoghurt
6 ice cubes

serves 1–2

Put all the ingredients in a blender and then blend until smooth.

Fruit juice ice cubes melt more slowly than regular ice and inject a gradual essence of fruit into other ingredients, such as yoghurt or buttermilk. This recipe is especially delicious – yoghurt with honey is one of those marriages made in heaven.

fruit ice cubes
with yoghurt & honey

1 litre/4 cups fresh fruit juice, such as cranberry or apricot
sugar, to taste (optional)
750 ml/3 cups low-fat yoghurt
honey, to serve

serves 4

Sweeten the fruit juice if preferred, then freeze in ice cube trays.

Fill glasses with the fruit ice cubes and spoon in the yoghurt. Drizzle a few spoonfuls of honey over the top and serve.

raspberry yogurt smoothie

Yoghurt, whether low-fat or full-cream, is one of nature's wonder foods. It is one of the best ways to add calcium to the diet – especially important for women.

raspberry yoghurt smoothie

1 punnet/basket raspberries, about 250 g/2 cups
6–8 ice cubes
250 ml/1 cup low-fat yoghurt
sparkling mineral water or low-fat milk
mild honey or sugar, to taste (optional)

serves 4

Put the raspberries in a blender with the ice cubes, yoghurt and enough sparkling mineral water or milk to make the machine run. Blend to a thin froth, adding more water or milk as required.

Taste and add honey or sugar if using, then serve.

This drink is almost thick enough to pour into a glass, chill and serve as dessert; it is certainly tasty enough. As always, rosewater adds a hint of the exotic and will have people guessing.

rhubarb, yoghurt & rosewater smoothie

200 g/7 oz. trimmed rhubarb
3 tablespoons honey
250 ml/1 cup organic low-fat yoghurt
250 ml/1 cup organic skimmed milk
1 tablespoon rosewater

serves 2

Cut the rhubarb into 5 cm/2 inch lengths and put in a saucepan with 2 tablespoons water and the honey. Bring slowly to the boil and simmer gently for 5–8 minutes until softened. Set aside until completely cold.

Put the cooled rhubarb mixture in a blender with the remaining ingredients and blend until smooth.

Even people with dairy intolerance are often able to eat yoghurt, since it changes its structure during fermentation. It's marvellous for upset stomachs too!

red berry smoothie

1 punnet/basket berries (about 250 g/2 cups), such as strawberries, cranberries, redcurrants or raspberries (for a pink smoothie), or blackberries and blueberries (for a blue smoothie)

250 ml/1 cup plain yoghurt

125 ml/½ cup crushed ice

sugar or honey, to taste

serves 2–3

If using strawberries, hull them. Put all the ingredients except the sugar or honey in a blender and work to a thin, frothy cream. If too thick, add water to create a pourable consistency. Taste, then add sugar or honey if preferred.

LEFT *strawberry fruche*
RIGHT *frozen berry smoothie*

A fresh-tasting shake made with fromage frais (also known as fromage blanc), a fresh, soft cheese. Pure fromage frais is virtually fat free but often contains added cream, so check the label if you are cutting down on fat. If you can't find fromage frais, you can use Greek yoghurt instead.

strawberry fruche

250 g/2 cups strawberries, plus extra sliced strawberries to serve

250 ml/1 cup plain fromage frais

1 teaspoon ground cinnamon, plus extra to serve

300 ml/1¼ cups organic milk

serves 2

Hull the strawberries, put them in a blender with the fromage frais, cinnamon and milk and blend until smooth. Serve topped with strawberry slices and a sprinkling of cinnamon.

Frozen berries are great for blended drinks as they are available year round and can be blended straight from the freezer, making the drink thick and instantly chilled. This is a great one for kids – how many do you know who don't like berries and ice cream?

frozen berry smoothie

150 g/1¼ cups frozen mixed berries

2 scoops vanilla ice cream

500 ml/2 cups organic milk

serves 2

Put all the ingredients in a blender and then blend until smooth.

This is such a rich, indulgent drink it could be served as a summer dessert. For a more chunky texture – think gooey meringue – blend for just a short burst.

Eton mess

250 g strawberries or raspberries, or a mixture of both

2 meringues, about 65 g/2½ oz.

125 ml/½ cup single/light cream

250 ml/1 cup organic milk

1 teaspoon vanilla extract

serves 3–4

If using strawberries, hull them. Put all the ingredients in a blender and blend until smooth.

Strawberry smoothies are invariably the most popular with guests. Serve them made just with ice, or with yoghurt, ice cream or milk. Or (as here) with the lot: self-indulgence is a very good thing.

strawberry ice cream smoothie

12 ice cubes

4 scoops strawberry ice cream

12 large ripe strawberries, hulled and halved

125 ml/½ cup low-fat yoghurt

low-fat milk

serves 4

Put the ice cubes in a blender and blend to a snow. Add the ice cream, strawberries and yoghurt and blend again, adding enough milk to give a creamy consistency. Pour into glasses and serve.

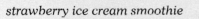
strawberry ice cream smoothie

In South-east Asia, street vendors sell plastic bags filled with drinks – often luridly coloured. They are sealed and a straw provided to pierce the bag. Condensed milk is a common ingredient, used to add sweetness and creaminess to the mixture. Use plain cream if you prefer.

thai papaya smoothie
with mint, lime & condensed milk

10 ice cubes

1 papaya, peeled, halved and deseeded

freshly squeezed juice of 1 lime

3 tablespoons condensed milk

6 fresh mint leaves

serves 2

Put the ice cubes in the blender and work to a snow. Chop the papaya flesh and add to the blender. Add the lime juice, condensed milk and mint leaves, blend again, then serve.

Lassis are a traditional yoghurt drink in India, served plain, sweet or salty – perfect coolers in hot weather. This is a very indulgent form of lassi, but you can take refuge in the fact that yoghurt and ginger are very calming for upset stomachs. Use low-fat yoghurt if you prefer, and substitute almost any fruit you have on hand, including non-tropical ones like pears, apricots or peaches.

tropical fruit lassi
with papaya ginger & lime

250 ml/1 cup peeled, deseeded papaya

250 ml/1 cup crushed pineapple or pineapple juice

1 banana

250–500 ml/1–2 cups plain yoghurt

1 tablespoon puréed fresh ginger (see note on page 215)

freshly squeezed juice and grated zest of 1 lime

crushed ice, to serve

sprigs of fresh mint, to garnish

serves 2–3

Place all the ingredients in a blender or food processor and purée. Serve poured over crushed ice and garnished with mint.

This tasty tropical lassi has hidden health benefits. Aromatic cardamom is a traditional digestive aid, while bio yoghurt and the form of fibre found in bananas may help the natural balance of the digestive system.

tropical fruit & cardamom lassi

4 green cardamom pods

1 mango

2 bananas, peeled and thickly sliced

100 ml/scant ½ cup canned reduced-fat coconut milk

150 ml/⅔ cup thick, low-fat bio yoghurt

150 ml/⅔ cup semi-skimmed milk

ice cubes, to serve

serves 2

Crush the cardamom pods and remove the seeds, then grind them to a coarse powder with a pestle and mortar.

Cut the mango in half either side of the central stone. Taking the 2 halves, cut the flesh into a criss-cross pattern down to the skin. Press each half inside out, then cut the mango cubes away from the skin. Put the cardamom in a blender with the mango, bananas, coconut milk, yoghurt and milk, then blend until smooth and frothy – you may need to do this in 2 batches. Put ice cubes in 2 tall glasses and top up with the lassi.

This non-alcoholic version of the classic cocktail is delightfully indulgent, as well as a source of protein, vitamins and minerals.

no-booze piña colada

1 papaya

1 small pineapple

1 banana, peeled and thickly sliced

200 ml/¾ cup canned reduced-fat coconut milk

150 ml/⅔ cup thick, low-fat bio yoghurt

serves 2

Cut the papaya in half, then scoop out the seeds with a spoon. Peel the papaya and cut into chunks. Cut the pineapple lengthways into quarters, then cut away the skin, remove the core and cut the flesh into chunks.

Put the papaya, pineapple and banana in a blender with the coconut milk and yoghurt, then blend until smooth and creamy – you may have to do this in 2 batches.

vegetable juices

LEFT *middle eastern delight*

CENTRE *breakfast zinger*
(recipe on page 178)

RIGHT *hangover cure*

This nutrient-rich juice is a true pick-me-up, and will help revitalize, hydrate, nourish and cleanse. Tomatoes can help protect against cancer, while cucumber hydrates the body, especially when counteracting the effects of alcohol. Lemongrass acts to aid digestion and soothes nausea.

hangover cure

2 small ripe tomatoes,
about 175 g/6 oz.

125 g/4½ oz. cucumber

2 celery stalks, trimmed

½ red bell pepper, cored and
deseeded

½ lemongrass stalk

½ long red chilli, cored and
deseeded

a wedge of cucumber or ½ celery
stalk, to serve

serves 1

Cut everything into chunks and press through a juicer into a large glass. Serve immediately with a long wedge of cucumber or half a celery stalk.

This wonderful rose-coloured juice is an immune-system tonic. Traditionally the juices of carrots, oranges and pomegranates were used as a preventative against cancer, due to their high antioxidant content.

middle eastern delight

2 carrots

2 oranges

1 pomegranate, about 350 g/12 oz.

a few drops of rosewater

serves 1–2

Cut the carrots into chunks. Peel the oranges and cut the flesh into chunks. Press the oranges and carrots through a juicer into a jug/pitcher.

Cut the pomegranate in half. Using a citrus squeezer, extract as much juice as possible. Strain through a sieve/strainer into the jug/pitcher. Add the rosewater and stir well.

This tangy juice is a great morning cleanser. Lemons cleanse and aid digestion of the other vegetables. Beetroot helps reduce high blood cholesterol levels, and, as it has a very low glycaemic index, keeps blood sugar levels stable. Beta-carotene-rich carrot eliminates toxins, while the apple adds fibre and sweetness.

breakfast zinger

1 lemon

1 beetroot/beet, about 150 g/5½ oz., trimmed and scrubbed

1 carrot

1 apple

serves 1

Peel the lemon, discarding the white pith, and cut the flesh into chunks. Cut the beetroot/beet, carrot and apple into chunks that will easily fit into the funnel on your juicer and press everything through into a large glass.

pictured on page 176

This wonderful juice is called Dark Surprise due to its fantastic deep purple colour, from the beetroot and blackberries. Don't be deterred by this unusual combination; it is truly delicious, sweet and very refreshing, and is also an excellent remedy for cystitis.

dark surprise

2 beetroot/beets, about 300 g/10½ oz., trimmed and scrubbed

150 g/1¼ cups frozen blackberries

250 ml/1 cup cranberry juice

serves 2–3

Cut the beetroot/beets into chunks small enough to fit through the funnel on your juicer, then press through into a jug/pitcher. Transfer to a blender, add the blackberries and cranberry juice and blend until smooth.

dark surprise

Carrot juice, so naturally sweet, makes a great basis for juices, like this one with the added zing of ginger. Just make sure you peel them first, unless they have been organically grown. Carrots are high in beta-carotene, which the body uses to convert into vitamin A.

carrot & ginger crush

5 carrots, peeled
a chunk of fresh ginger, peeled and sliced

serves 1–2

Cut the carrots into pieces small enough to fit through the funnel on your juicer. When half the carrots have been processed, add the ginger, then the rest of the carrots.

note
Don't drink carrot juice more than 2–3 times a week, otherwise your skin may develop an orange, carroty tinge!

Celery juice is marvellous when mixed with other vegetable juices – and also with juicy fruits such as grapes. You can buy grape juice, but fresh juice is a revelation. White grapes will produce a fresh green juice, red or black ones a delicious pink-tinged nectar. Celery has almost no calories – it's like eating water, so is marvellous for dieters. Celery is also a natural tranquilizer, so sip and snooze.

celery & grape juice

6 celery stalks, trimmed
about 20 seedless white grapes
1 bunch watercress (optional)
ice cubes

serves 1–2

Push the celery stalks into the juicer, leaf end first. Alternate with the grapes, which are very soft and difficult to push through on their own. Press through the watercress, if using, and serve plain, in glasses filled with ice, or blend in a blender with ice cubes to produce a delicious celery-grape froth.

celery, carrot & pineapple refresher

This fruit and vegetable juice is the perfect digestive aid to drink half an hour before you eat. It is a good anti-nausea remedy in cases of pregnancy, travel sickness or vertigo. Ginger and peppermint help a fever, while pineapple acts as an anti-inflammatory in fever, sinusitis and arthritis.

celery, carrot & pineapple refresher

½ small pineapple, about
550 g/1 lb. 4 oz.
3 celery stalks, trimmed
2 carrots
a small piece fresh ginger, peeled
leaves from 2 sprigs of fresh mint
ice cubes, to serve

serves 2

Peel the pineapple, remove the tough central core and cut the flesh into chunks. Cut the celery stalks and carrots into chunks. Press all the ingredients through a juicer into a jug/pitcher and serve over ice.

A vegetable cocktail that is a valuable source of vitamins, minerals and antioxidants, especially when you've had to skip a meal or when you need extra nutrients, for example during an illness or period of stress.

salad in a glass

2 small oranges, about 350 g/12 oz.
200 g/7 oz. cos/romaine or
butter lettuce
1 green bell pepper, cored and
deseeded
2 green apples
125 g/4½ oz. cucumber
½ bunch parsley leaves

serves 3

Peel the oranges and cut the flesh into smallish chunks. Cut the lettuce, pepper, apples and cucumber into pieces small enough to fit through the funnel on your juicer. Press all the ingredients through the juicer into a jug/pitcher.

A potent hydrator and thirst-quencher, the cooling cucumber and refreshing mint stimulate the palate and help rid the digestive system of toxins. The naturally rich sugars found in melon and grapes will provide you with a burst of energy. Cucumber is an excellent diuretic, and being rich in silicon is beneficial for hair, skin and nails.

wake up & go juice

½ lemon
a small wedge honeydew melon, about 175 g/6 oz., deseeded and peeled
½ cucumber
1 celery stalk
100 g/¾ cup green grapes
a handful of fresh mint leaves

serves 1

Peel the lemon, discarding the white pith, and cut the flesh into chunks. Cut the melon flesh, cucumber and celery into chunks. Press all the ingredients through a juicer into a jug/pitcher or large glass.

Drinking spinach juice is no-one's idea of a good time, but mix it with something more delicious and you'll absorb all its goodness almost painlessly. Apple or cucumber are both good choices. If using cucumbers, try to use organically grown produce. Others are often waxed and must be peeled first (so you lose some of the colour and nutrients).

cucumber juice with spinach

1 organic cucumber, about 30 cm/12 inches long, quartered lengthways
a large handful of well-washed spinach
salt or lemon juice, to taste (optional)

serves 1–2

Juice half the cucumber, then all the spinach, then the remaining cucumber. Add salt or lemon juice to taste, if preferred.

variation
Cucumber has a cooling, astringent effect – to sweeten it, use half-and-half with apple juice from crisp Granny Smiths.

This is an overall health tonic that promotes regular bowel motions and the elimination of mucus. Ginger helps to clear mucus from the sinuses and acts as a digestive, so this drink is both stimulating and calming. Fennel helps to remedy liver stagnancy and also acts as a digestive.

autumn crumble

1 apple

1 pear

1 large carrot, about 200 g/7 oz.

1 fennel bulb, about 175 g/6 oz., trimmed

1 cm/½ inch piece fresh ginger

serves 1

Cut the apple, pear, carrot and fennel into chunks that will fit into the funnel on your juicer. Press all the ingredients through the juicer into a large glass.

This lip-smacking juice is a potent digestive aid. It will help purge the bowels and clear the sinuses. Best served in shot glasses for an instant kick-start to your day.

ginger spice

½ lemon

1 fennel bulb, about 175 g/6 oz., trimmed

1 apple

2.5 cm/1 inch piece fresh ginger

100 g/¾ cup green grapes

serves 3

Peel the lemon, discarding the white pith, and cut the flesh into chunks. Cut the fennel and apple into smallish chunks and then press all the ingredients through a juicer into a jug/pitcher.

LEFT *autumn crumble*
RIGHT *ginger spice*

Lettuce and parsley produce small quantities of juice and taste decidedly green! So add the juice of an apple or other fruit as an extender and sweetener. As many good cooks know, much of the flavour in parsley is in the stalks, so juice them too. Before juicing, all leafy vegetables should be washed well, wrapped in a cloth and chilled until crisp.

lettuce & parsley crush

1 cos/romaine or iceberg lettuce, stalk trimmed

1 large bunch parsley, including stalks, ends trimmed

1 green apple, cored and quartered, but not peeled

serves 1

Form the lettuce and parsley leaves into balls and push through the funnel on your juicer. Push the apple through (this will extract more juice from the lettuce and parsley). Stir if necessary, then serve immediately – don't wait.

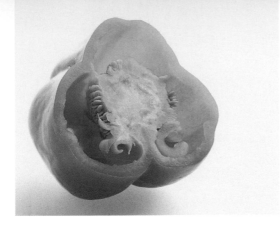

Peppers, tomatoes and chillies originally came from Mexico. You can vary the heat to your own taste, adding more chilli or using a hotter variety. The pinch of salt is optional, but salt will point up the flavour beautifully, or try a dash of lemon juice instead. Peppers and their hot-headed chilli cousins have three times as much vitamin C as an orange. Juicing removes the skins and extracts all the sweet flavour.

mexican golden salsa crush

2 red, orange or yellow bell peppers, cored and deseeded

1 medium-hot red chilli, deseeded

2 tomatoes, quartered

a pinch of salt or a squeeze of lemon juice (optional)

ice cubes, to serve (optional)

serves 1

Push 1 pepper through the juicer, then the chilli, tomatoes and salt or lemon juice, if using. Push through the remaining pepper and serve immediately, over ice, if preferred.

Make Bloody Mary with fresh tomato juice, as it is thinner and sweeter than the commercial kinds – and more delicious. The tomato is probably the world's single most wonderful vegetable (though it's technically a fruit). Tomatoes are low in calories but high in vitamins C and E, plus potassium, beta-carotene and lycopene, which helps some forms of cancer by preventing damage by free radicals.

fresh virgin mary

6 ripe tomatoes
3 celery stalks
1 garlic clove (optional)
1 red chilli, deseeded
ice cubes
a dash of Worcestershire sauce
(optional)

serves 1

To skin the tomatoes, cut a small cross in the base, put in a large heat-proof bowl and cover with boiling water. Leave for 1 minute, then drain and pull off the skins. Juice the tomatoes, celery, garlic, if using, and chilli. Pour into a jug/pitcher of ice, stir in the Worcestershire sauce, if using, then serve (with or without vodka).

variation
Add other fruit and vegetable juices such as broccoli, cabbage, lemon or radish – and a dash of Moroccan harissa paste.

fruit with a kick

Martinis never tasted or looked so good! Each fruit quantity will make four drinks, so choose whichever flavour you prefer – or why not try one of each?

fruit martinis

250 g/9 oz. kiwi fruit (about 4 kiwi fruit)

250 g/2 cups strawberries, hulled

250 g/9 oz. deseeded and peeled watermelon

3 tablespoons caster/superfine sugar

240 ml/1 cup iced vodka

kiwi fruit slices, strawberries and small watermelon wedges, to garnish

ice cubes, lightly crushed, to serve

serves 4–12, as desired

Purée each fruit separately in a blender or liquidizer with 1 tablespoon sugar until really smooth and then set aside.

Put each fruit purée separately into a cocktail shaker and add 80 ml/⅓ cup iced vodka and a little crushed ice. Replace the lid and shake vigorously for about 30 seconds, remove the lid and pour into 4 martini glasses. Decorate each glass with a slice of the fruit used in the martini and serve immediately.

A delicious drink based on sloe gin, which is made in autumn from the fruit of the blackthorn, then set aside until Christmas. Blueberries make a worthy substitute. It should be served in small glasses – it tastes wonderful, but is very heady, and can be something of a trap. You can also serve it in long glasses with ice and tonic water. Delicious and the most marvellous colour!

blueberry gin

1 punnet/basket blueberries, about 250 g/2 cups
6 tablespoons sugar
1 large bottle gin, 750 ml/3 cups

to serve
crushed ice (optional)
tonic water (optional)
sprigs of fresh mint (optional)

serves 15–20

Put the blueberries in a large glass bottle or empty bottle of spirits. Add the sugar and gin, then shake well and set aside for at least 2 weeks, or up to 2 months. Shake the bottle from time to time – you will see the marvellous rich colour developing as the days go by.

Put a shot of the gin in a blender with 3 tablespoons crushed ice. Blend, then pour into long chilled glasses. Add a sprig of mint and tonic to taste. Alternatively, serve alone in small aquavit-style or shot glasses. Do not drive!

A wonderful drink for a summer brunch party. Serve in a huge glass jug so guests can help themselves. Use ruby grapefruit if you can find them – 2–3 juicy ones will produce this amount of juice. Campari isn't very intoxicating, so this is a perfect drink for early in the day – and great as a pre-dinner drink in summer too.

ruby grapefruit Campari whizz

250 ml/1 cup crushed ice, plus extra
to serve
4 tablespoons Campari, or to taste
500 ml/2 cups freshly squeezed ruby
grapefruit juice, chilled
sprigs of fresh mint, to serve

serves 2–4

Whizz the crushed ice with the Campari and grapefruit juice in a blender. Half-fill a jug/pitcher with more crushed ice, pour in the mixture, cram the top of the jug/pitcher with mint sprigs and serve.

Honey and pears go wonderfully together, and are combined here in this sweet, refreshing cocktail. If you are lucky enough to find nashi pears, which are a lovely combination of apples and pears, try those, but don't worry if not, normal pears work very well too.

iced pear sparkle

1 teaspoon honey

2 tablespoons pear liqueur

2 tablespoons Cointreau or other orange-flavoured liqueur

¼ pear (nashi if available), peeled, cored and thinly sliced

Champagne or sparkling white wine

ice cubes, to serve

serves 1

Put the honey and some ice in a cocktail shaker and gently crush with a wooden muddler. Add the pear and orange liqueurs, replace the lid and shake briskly but briefly.

Pour into a chilled glass, add some pear slices and top up with Champagne or sparkling white wine. Serve immediately.

mandarin caprioska

Although mandarin season is traditionally winter, like lemons and limes, mandarins are now available most of the year. So this is actually the perfect summertime barbecue cocktail – it seems to work well with smoky char-grilled food. When mandarins are unavailable, you can use tangerines or even oranges.

mandarin caprioska

1 mandarin, cut into wedges
fresh mint leaves, torn
2 tablespoons triple sec
2 tablespoons vodka
tonic water, to top up
ice cubes, to serve

serves 1

Put the mandarin wedges, mint leaves and ice in a chilled glass, squeezing the mandarin wedges as you go to release their juices. Pour over the triple sec and vodka, then top up with tonic water to serve.

Rum has a great affinity with fresh juices and the ability to hold its own when combined with quite a selection of other flavours. This delicious long drink is packed with fruity cranberry and pineapple juices and given a bit of extra zing with spicy fresh ginger.

Jamaican breeze

50 ml/¼ cup white rum
2 slices fresh ginger, peeled
75 ml/⅓ cup cranberry juice
75 ml/⅓ cup fresh pineapple juice
ice cubes, to serve

serves 1

Put the rum and ginger together in the bottom of a cocktail shaker and pound with a wooden muddler. Add ice to the shaker and pour in the cranberry and pineapple juices. Shake briskly, then strain into a tall glass filled with ice. Serve immediately.

Kumquats, sometimes called Chinese oranges, are small, tasty citrus fruits. Contrary to most members of the citrus family, it is the outside peel of the kumquat that is sweet, while the inside flesh is rather tart.

lobby dazzler

3–4 kumquats, quartered
2 teaspoons sugar
50 ml/⅓ cup Absolut Kurant vodka
crushed ice, to serve

serves 1

Put the kumquats in an old-fashioned glass and sprinkle with the sugar. Using a pestle or the back of a spoon, crush the kumquat and sugar together until the sugar completely dissolves and all the fruit juice is released.

Fill the glass with crushed ice, add the vodka and stir briefly before serving.

While slushies are usually enjoyed by children, this fruity iced treat is definitely one for the adults, and is really worth that little bit of extra effort.

cider apple slushie

3 large cooking apples, peeled, cored and sliced, plus extra thin slices to garnish (optional)
1 litre/4 cups sweet cider
250 g/1¼ cups sugar
2 cinnamon sticks, lightly bashed

serves 4

Put the apples, cider, sugar and cinnamon sticks in a saucepan and bring slowly to the boil, stirring until the sugar has dissolved. Cover and simmer gently for 12–15 minutes until the apples are soft.

Remove from the heat and leave to cool. When cool, remove the cinnamon sticks and discard. Transfer the mixture to a blender or liquidizer. Whizz until smooth, then spoon into a freezerproof container and freeze for 4–6 hours.

To serve, return the mixture to the blender and whizz briefly. Pour into tall glasses, garnish with apple slices, if using, and serve immediately.

Kir Royale is cassis with champagne. This party drink is a mango and ginger version. If you can find it, canned Indian Alphonso mango purée works very well, but you can also use frozen mango – blended while still frozen to an icy purée – or fresh mango. If using frozen or fresh mangoes, you'll have to add a little lemon juice to develop the flavour and ice to help smash the fibre.

mango & ginger kir royale

1 jar preserved stem ginger in syrup, pieces cut into quarters, or crystallized ginger

500 ml/2 cups mango purée

8 tablespoons ginger purée* or juice

syrup from the jar of stem ginger (optional)

sugar, to taste

6 x 750 ml bottles chilled champagne (8 glasses per bottle for champagne cocktails)

makes at least 50 glasses

Thread the quarter pieces of ginger, lengthways, onto the end of a long cocktail stick or bamboo skewer. Arrange them on a plate or in a bowl, ginger ends downward.

Working in batches if necessary, put the mango purée in a blender, add the ginger purée or juice, the syrup from the jar, if using, and 250 ml/1 cup iced water. Blend well. Add sugar to taste. Blend again, then add more iced water until the mixture is the texture of thin cream – if it's too thick it will fall to the bottom of the glass.

Arrange champagne flutes on serving trays, then put 1 teaspoon of the mango mixture into each one. Add a small teaspoon of champagne, stir and set aside until your guests arrive. When they do, top up the glasses with champagne (twice, because they bubble like mad), then put a ginger cocktail stick across the top of each one and tell your guests it's a swizzle stick. They will want more, so have extra mango mixture ready.

*note
Ginger purée is sold in jars in some supermarkets. To make your own, cut 1 kg/2¼ lb. fresh ginger into pieces about 5 cm/2 inches long. Soak in water to cover for about 30 minutes, then peel and chop coarsely. Transfer to a blender or spice grinder and work to a purée. You may need to add a little iced water or lemon juice. You can press the juice through a sieve/strainer or freeze the pulp in ice cube trays, then use in this and other recipes as needed. You'll need at least 8 cubes for this recipe.

Many Caribbean punches are very strong, and this is one of them. You can also serve it as a less-fiery party punch, served in a punch bowl and topped up with mixers.

mango rum punch

250 ml/1 cup mango purée or
250 g/9 oz. frozen mango
1 teaspoon freshly squeezed
lemon juice
a pinch of ground cardamom*
500 ml/2 cups golden rum
6 ice cubes, plus extra to serve
black seeds from 3 cardamom pods*

serves 10

Put the mango or mango purée in a blender with the lemon juice, ground cardamom and rum. Add the ice cubes and blend until smooth. Strain into chilled glasses, filled with ice if preferred, and top with a few cardamom seeds.

*note
For the best cardamom, crush 6 green pods with a mortar and pestle, extract the black seeds and discard the green pods. Grind the pods to a powder using the mortar and pestle.

This punch has a distinctly Caribbean feel. You could use golden rum, but white rum gives a slightly more delicate flavour.

passion fruit rum punch

300 ml/1¼ cups white rum

150 ml/⅔ cup passion fruit pulp and seeds (from about 6 large ripe passion fruit)

150 ml/⅔ cup freshly squeezed orange juice

600 ml/2½ cups clear sparkling lemonade

ice cubes, to serve

serves 6

Put the rum, passion fruit pulp and orange juice in a large jug/pitcher and chill for 1 hour.

Half-fill 6 tall glasses with ice, add the rum and fruit juice mixture and top up with sparkling lemonade. Serve immediately.

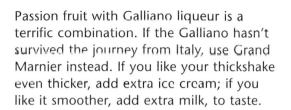

Passion fruit with Galliano liqueur is a terrific combination. If the Galliano hasn't survived the journey from Italy, use Grand Marnier instead. If you like your thickshake even thicker, add extra ice cream; if you like it smoother, add extra milk, to taste.

passion fruit thickshake
with Galliano

3 passionfruit, chilled
1 tablespoon Galliano
3 scoops vanilla ice cream
100 ml milk/scant ½ cup, or to taste
sugar, to taste

serves 1–2

Scoop the pulp and seeds of 2 passion fruit into the blender, add the Galliano, ice cream and milk, then blend.

Taste, then add sugar and a little extra milk if preferred. Spoon the remaining passion fruit over the top, then serve.

A fragrant and more delicate version of the Spanish classic sangria. You can add almost any fruit you like and vary the liqueur. Try peach schnapps or crème de framboise (raspberry-flavoured liqueur).

peach & strawberry sangria

2 fresh peaches, stoned and thinly sliced

250 g/2 cups strawberries, hulled and sliced

1 orange, sliced

150 ml/⅔ cup Crème de Fraise (strawberry-flavoured liqueur)

2 x 750 ml bottles dry white wine

1 small cucumber, peeled, deseeded and thinly sliced

clear sparkling lemonade, to top up

borage flowers, to garnish (optional)

ice cubes, to serve

serves 12

Put the peaches, strawberries and orange slices in a large jug/pitcher with the strawberry liqueur. Pour in the wine and chill for 30 minutes. When ready to serve, add the cucumber and some ice and top up with lemonade. Pour into glasses and garnish each serving with borage flowers, if using.

For this recipe, try and use golden rum. Although dark rum is richer in flavour, it isn't such a pretty colour when used with ingredients like these, so instead use a golden rum from Barbados or one of the other Caribbean islands. You could also use white rum, but it doesn't have the depth of flavour of the darker ones.

pineapple rum

500 ml/2 cups fresh pineapple juice
or 1 ripe pineapple, peeled and cored

2 tablespoons ginger purée
or 2 pieces preserved ginger in syrup,
to taste

250 ml/1 cup golden rum or
white rum

ginger beer or ginger ale (optional)

serves 4–6

Whizz the pineapple juice or flesh in a blender with the ginger purée or preserved ginger and syrup. Strain into a tall jug/pitcher of ice. Stir in the rum and serve immediately, or top with ginger beer or ginger ale. Alternatively, strain into tall glasses full of ice, and top with ginger beer or ginger ale.

Cranberry juice lends a light, fruity quality to this classic cocktail. Slightly bitter, it is very refreshing served ice cold on a warm day.

sea breeze

30 ml/2 tablespoons vodka
150 ml/⅔ cup cranberry juice
50 ml/¼ cup freshly squeezed grapefruit juice
a lime wedge, to garnish
ice cubes, to serve

serves 1

Half-fill a tall glass with ice. Pour in the vodka and add the cranberry and grapefruit juices. Stir and garnish with a lime wedge. Serve immediately.

The dry taste of the cranberry juice is softened by the triple sec in this pretty pink cocktail. Do try it with vanilla vodka, if available, as it makes it all the sweeter.

cosmopolitan iced tea

30 ml/2 tablespoons vodka, vanilla-flavoured if available
15 ml/1 tablespoon triple sec
75 ml/⅓ cup cranberry juice
freshly squeezed juice of ½ lime
ice cubes, to serve

serves 1

Fill a cocktail shaker with ice. Add the vodka, triple sec and cranberry and lime juices. Replace the lid and shake briskly. Strain into a tall glass, half-filled with ice. Serve immediately.

Old-time American soda jerks were experts at balancing a scoop of ice cream on the edge of the soda glass. If you're not, you could always try to balance yours on a teaspoon! Make endless variations of this recipe, matching the liqueur to the fruit – crème de fraise with strawberries, crème de framboise with raspberries, Poire William with pears, peach liqueur with peaches, and so on.

strawberry liqueur smoothie

250 g/2 cups strawberries, hulled
1 tablespoon strawberry liqueur
3 scoops strawberry ice cream, plus
an extra small scoop, to serve
100 ml/scant ½ cup milk, or to taste

serves 1–2

Place all the ingredients in a blender and whizz. Add extra ice cream for a thicker smoothie, or extra milk, to taste. Serve in a soda glass with an extra small scoop of ice cream balanced on the edge of the glass (if possible).

variation: Strawberry Spider
Take a tall glass and add a scoop of strawberry ice cream and 1 tablespoon liqueur or strawberry syrup, then top up with soda (preferably strawberry). Pour in the soda very carefully – it will fizz like mad!

This tropical crush is so thick and wonderful it's almost a soup. It serves one as a smoothie, and about six people as a champagne cocktail. Don't forget to chill all the fruits first – but wrap up the very aromatic ones in cling film/plastic wrap to prevent them tainting the other foods in your refrigerator.

thick tropical crush

tropical fruits such as:
250 g/9 oz. cubed fresh papaya
250 g/9 oz. cubed fresh pineapple
chilled Champagne (see method)
sugar, to taste (optional)
watermelon triangles, to serve

serves 1 or 6

Whizz the fruits in the blender with 125 ml/½ cup champagne. Add sugar to taste, if using. Pour into a chilled glass, and serve with watermelon triangles threaded onto cocktail sticks. Alternatively, divide between 6 glasses, top with Champagne, and serve as Champagne cocktails.

Spanish sangria with a South American twist! Use any fruit, but include tropicals, like mango, pineapple or star fruit. Don't use any that go 'furry', such as melon or strawberries. This is great for a summer party in the garden, and you can produce a non-alcoholic kind for children and non-drinkers using ginger ale or lemonade instead of the Champagne.

tropical sangria

1 ripe mango, stoned and finely sliced

1 lime, finely sliced

1 lemon, finely sliced

½ pineapple, peeled, cored and finely sliced

3 kiwi fruit, sliced

1 star fruit (carambola), sliced

3 tablespoons caster/superfine sugar

1 x 750 ml bottle Champagne, chilled

serves 4–8

Put all the fruit in a punch bowl, sprinkle with sugar and set aside for 30 minutes. Top with icy Champagne just before serving.

variations: Quick Neapolitan Sangria
Half-fill a punch bowl with ice, add 1 bottle orange squash and 2 bottles light red wine.

Neapolitan Red Peach Sangria
Half-fill a punch bowl with ice, add 1 bottle light red wine, 250 ml/1 cup peach nectar, mint sprigs and 1 sliced peach.

The summery flavour of ripe, red watermelon goes wonderfully well with the fresh, clean, lemony taste of gin. But do remember to deseed the watermelon before blending or the seeds can make the drink taste bitter.

watermelon gin

2 very ripe watermelons, well chilled
500–750 ml/2–3 cups gin, or to taste

to serve
crushed ice
sprigs of fresh mint
watermelon triangles, to serve (optional)

serves 10–20

Cut the watermelon in half and remove the seeds and skin. Working in batches, put the flesh in a blender or food processor and blend until smooth. If the mixture is too thick, add water.

Pour into a jug/pitcher and stir in the gin. Fill glasses with ice, pour over the Watermelon Gin and serve topped with a sprig of mint and a melon triangle.

variation: Lime & Watermelon Vodka
Substitute vodka instead of the gin, and stir in the juice of 2 freshly squeezed limes.

index

recipe credits

Elsa Petersen-Schepelern
apple lemonade
apple juice with fennel
apricot ice cream smoothie with cream
banana & honey breakfast smoothie
banana & papaya smoothie
banana & peanut butter smoothie
berry, apricot & orange slush
berry ice blocks with buttermilk froth
blueberry gin
blueberry ice cream smoothie
blueberry & orange smoothie
breakfast shake with dried apricots
carrot & ginger crush
celery & grapes
cherry-chocolate smoothie with frozen cherries stuffed with M&Ms
coconut banana shake
coconut milk smoothie with vanilla, peaches & lime
cranberry cooler
cucumber juice with spinach
dried pear & mint froth
fresh virgin mary
frozen fruit juice granitas
frozen watermelon, ginger & lime
fruit ice cubes with yoghurt & honey
fruit salad lassi with strawberries
gingered pear juice
ginger shake
Indian frozen lime with soda
lettuce & parsley crush
mango & ginger kir royale
mango & ginger lassi with low-fat yoghurt
mango rum punch
mango smoothie with strawberries & soy milk
melon froth
Mexican golden salsa crush
minty ginger granny smith
passion fruit meringue smoothie
passion fruit thickshake with Galliano
pineapple crush
pineapple ginger smoothie
pineapple rum
pineapple & strawberry crush
pomegranate squeeze
raspberry smoothie with soy milk
raspberry yoghurt smoothie
red berry smoothie
rhubarb strawberryade
ruby grapefruit campari whizz
strawberry ice cream smoothie
strawberry juice with balsamic
strawberry liqueur smoothie
strawberry slush with mango & lime
strawberry smoothie with lime juice & mint
summer fruit crush
thai papaya smoothie with mint, lime & condensed milk
thick tropical crush
tropical fruit lassi with papaya, ginger & lime
tropical fruit smoothie with pineapple, watermelon, strawberries & lime
tropical sangria
vanilla or chocolate yoghurt lassi
watermelon & ginger sharbat

Louise Pickford
almond lassi
autumn classic
autumn crumble
avocado, pear & mint cooler
banana, nutmeg & honey smoothie
bananarama
berry boost
blueberry buzz
blueberry cordial with apple fizz
blueberry muesli smoothie
Bondi Rip
breakfast zinger
cardamom, coffee & date shake
celery, carrot & pineapple refresher
cherry berry crush
chilled lemongrass tisane
chocolate & banana cinnamon shake
cider apple slushie
cosmopolitan iced tea
dark surprise
elderflower & berry cup
Eton mess
frozen berry & banana blend
frozen berry smoothie
frozen cranberry, raspberry & grapefruit slushie
fruit bowl frappé
fruit martinis
ginger spice
go green juice
guava, strawberry & apple refresher
hangover cure
Iced Louisiana apricot tea
iced pear sparkle
jasmine & lychee iced tea
kick start your day
lemon cheesecake shake
malted milo shake
mandarin caprioska
mango & berry pash
mango, raspberry & cranberry cruise
mango & strawberry delight
melon, cucumber & sweet ginger frappé
middle eastern delight
mocha ice cream special
morning cleanser
orange & apple refresher
orange pear & banana breeze
papaya, melon & pear digestive
passion fruit rum punch
peach, apricot & plum fizz
peach melba ripple
peach & strawberry sangria
pineapple, ginger & mint slushie
pineapple & passion fruit soy shake
raspberry & apple fizz
raspberry, apple & lychee juice
rhubarb, yogurt & rosewater smoothie
roasted peaches & cream
salad in a glass
sea freeze
soy, sesame & maple syrup smoothie
spiced mango, coconut & lime smoothie
strawberry fruche
vanilla supreme
vitamin C boost juice
wake up & go juice
watermelon kick
watermelon & raspberry surprise
white chocolate frothy

Ben Reed
cranberry cooler
Jamaican breeze
sea breeze
St. Clements

Tonia George
basil limeade
chai vanilla milkshake
pineapple & mint agua fresca
pomegranate & orange sunrise

Fran Warde
lobby dazzler
melon & strawberry juice
super juice

Lyndel Costain & Nicola Grimes
almond & banana shake
citrus fizz
melon & ginger wake-up
no-booze pina colada
peach & orange nectar
strawberry & banana smoothie
tropical fruit & cardamom lassi

Brian Glover
homemade fresh lemonade

Maxine Clark
pear, apple & kiwifruit juice with fresh ginger
pussyfoot

photography credits

Jan Baldwin
Page 234

Martin Brigdale
Pages 73, 143, 217

Peters Cassidy
Pages 47, 64, 68, 71, 95, 110, 193, 206, 213, 214, 225, 230

Jean Cazals
Page 153

Dan Duchars
Page 130

Tara Fisher
Pages 36, 79, 146, 149, 222

Jonathan Gregson
Pages 7, 31, 70, 98

Richard Jung
Pages 3 left, 3 centre right, 52, 67, 72, 76, 189, 233

Sandra Lane
Page 210

Lisa Linder
Page 23

William Lingwood
Pages 3 centre left, 3 right, 10, 11, 21, 29, 34, 59, 65, 69, 75, 82, 84–90, 96, 97, 102, 103, 105, 109, 112, 113, 114, 144, 162, 163, 180-183, 188, 192, 194–197, 200, 207, 208, 212, 215, 218, 219, 223, 227

James Merrell
Pages 66, 101, 127, 132, 136, 152, 171, 203, 204, 216, 220, 224, 228, 231, 232, 235

Diana Miller
Page 201

David Montgomery
Pages 137, 170

David Munns
Page 32

Noel Murphy
Pages 78, 94, 125

William Reavell
Pages 35, 74, 93, 135, 172, 205, 229

Claire Richardson
Page 121

Debi Treloar
Pages 14, 22, 26, 33, 46, 50, 53, 54, 58, 62, 81, 117, 120, 128, 139, 147, 151, 159, 160, 167–169, 211, 221

Pia Tryde
Page 202

Ian Wallace
Pages 1, 2, 4–6, 8–9, 13, 17, 18, 25, 27, 28, 30, 37–42, 45, 49, 51, 57, 60–61, 63, 77, 104, 106, 108, 118–119, 123, 124, 126, 131,140, 145, 148, 155–158, 164, 174–179, 184, 187, 191, 198–199

Francesca Yorke
Pages 43, 91, 186